Crash Landing

Into a Field of

Outhouses

Vol. 1

*How $5 down
on a small airplane
brought him a lifetime
of excitement*

The Misguided Adventures of
Kenneth A. Bauer

Transcribed & Written
by Rochelle Cunningham

Best Wishes,
Ken Bauer
Rochelle Cunningham

2014

©2014 All rights reserved. No part of this publication may be reproduced or transmitted in any form or by any means, electronic or mechanical, including photocopying, recording, or by an information storage and retrieval system.

Any trademarks, service marks, product names or named features are used only for reference and are assumed to be the property of their respective owners, and the use of one of those terms does not imply endorsement on the part of the author and the publisher. In addition, every reasonable attempt has been made by the author and the publisher to achieve complete accuracy of the content in this publication.

A great deal of this publication is based on anecdotal information and personal experience. Remember that each person has a different set of life experiences. Your individual situation likely will have some differences from the examples given here. Please adapt your use of the information and suggestions accordingly.

In conclusion, remember that this publication is not meant to replace common sense, legal, medical or other advice. Put what is shared here in perspective with the other life lessons you have learned.

ISBN-13: 978-1497453753
ISBN-10: 1497453755

kabauer@me.com
boiserochelle@gmail.com

For Suzie and David ~

my fallen angels

Introduction

Welcome to the world of Kenneth A. Bauer and his many 'crash landings' throughout life. This collection of short stories invites the reader to a time when Americans experienced scarcity rather than the abundance we know today.

However, like many of his generation, Ken learned to create something out of nothing. He developed innovative, creative solutions for seemingly impossible scenarios and managed to maneuver through some sticky situations, escaping on a wing and a prayer.

Where Ken excelled was reinventing himself when times got tough; thus, resulting in multiple career changes and a variety of entertaining adventures. Ken accomplished many things in life with a positive attitude, an excellent work ethic, and by simply asking himself: *How tough could it be?*

Ken's childhood and young adult life spanned from the mid 1930's into the 1950's, so falling on hard times meant something entirely different back then. This never concerned him, because as far back as he can remember, Ken managed to find amusement in his world.

* * *

1939

Five year old Kenneth Bauer situated himself on the bottom step of his Omaha, Nebraska back porch on a warm Fourth of July evening. He was busy attempting to unravel the tightly laced ladyfinger firecrackers he'd convinced his dad to buy for him.

The amber sunset crawled along the length of the porch as Kenny watched Grandma Bauer prop the chicken-yard gate open so the hens could wander about in the twilight. Ken rested one of his Grandmother's cake pans on his lap and managed to separate a few of the ladyfingers from the tightly woven bundles.

The preoccupied boy paid little attention to the harsh voice he heard crackling from the radio inside the house, as it wafted out through an open window. He couldn't understand what the man was saying, or why his dad and grandfather were arguing about the strange man on the radio, he just thought "Hitler" was a really weird name.

Shrugging his shoulders, Kenny returned his attention to the cake pan. He struck a match with his uncoordinated little fingers, lit the end of the ladyfinger, and threw a single sizzling firework out into the yard.

sssssssPAP!

Kenny decided this was going to take forever. Then he got an idea!

Running into the house, he found one of his mother's candles that she kept under the kitchen sink. He returned to his cake pan, balancing it back onto his lap. He struck another match, lit the candle-wick, and placed the burning candle into the middle of the cake pan. Now he could pick up his firecrackers, light one at a time, and throw 'em at the chickens! This was much more exciting!

ssssssPAP! Burqcooock! Ken giggled at the fat little hens jumping and squawking at the noise. This was a lot of fun until his knees wobbled a little too far and the candle in Grandma's cake pan tipped over into the firecrackers. Kenny heard the hissing coming out of the pan and knew what was next! He jumped up from the steps, knocking the pan to the ground while firecrackers went off in every which direction!

sssssssPAP! PAP! PAP! PAP! PAP!

For what seemed like an eternity, the five year old ran around with the chickens, dodging firecrackers in the Bauer back yard.

This was only the beginning of Ken's curiosity with explosives. He would develop quite an appetite for chemistry in the years to come - and the poor chickens would continue to run scared!

* * *

This is one of many memories from Ken's wondrous childhood where his home and neighborhood served as marvelous playgrounds. Every day he woke into a world filled with endless possibilities and a collection of friends, family and neighbors to share in his adventures.

His curious and somewhat mischievous nature was cultivated within the walls of a multi-generational, German-influenced home in a rural area on the outskirts of Omaha, Nebraska. His neighbors consisted of low income families, most of which raised their own gardens and livestock.

The one and a half story Bauer house sat on an acre. The main floor had one bedroom, a living/dining room area, and a kitchen. The attic was used for two more small bedrooms.

The front yard had two large, black walnut trees, hackberry, and cherry trees that all shaded the south side. In the back yard was a weeping willow to shade the kitchen. Plum, apricot, and crabapple trees bordered the back yard along with lilac's that always sweetened the spring air. Several peach trees shaded the chicken-yard, which was near a large garden that grandpa maintained. A board covered path led from their two-hole outhouse to the back porch.

The south one-third of the acre was devoted to what Ken's grandpa called his "peony patch". Ken's dad and grandpa harvested the flowers, wrapped them in dozens, and put them in metal wash tubs with water. They took them down to 30th street, the main route to the large cemeteries such as Forest Lawn. Kenny loved to go along to help sell the flowers to people stopping to get bouquets to decorate their family's graves.

When someone pulled up to the curb for flowers, grandpa would ask, "Vat color you like?" then Kenny was allowed to deliver the bouquet to the car and collect the $1. He was a natural salesman and occasionally he was rewarded with a small tip. Later, whenever Ken smelled peonies blooming, he remembered those wonderful spring days with his dad and grandpa.

Ken also remembered the day his dad came home with a fabulous piece of technology that changed life as they knew it. It was a floor standing Philco radio, built of beautiful polished walnut. It had a piece of rectangular glass placed at an angle near the top, with a double hinged wood cover. Under the glass, were several lines with numbers on them and names like "Broadcast Band" and "Short Wave". There were four knurled, wheel-shaped controls to tune into the various stations. Kenny was only allowed to touch the one that controlled the pointer over the broadcast band.

Ken's little friends would join him in the afternoons, laying on the living room floor to listen to their programs.

They never missed *Jack Armstrong, the All American Boy*, and sent in their Wheaties cereal box tops for cardboard fighter planes. *Captain Midnight* was another favorite, and the boys would send in Ovaltine breakfast labels for secret decoder rings that would decode a preview of the next adventure!

The neighbors often joined Ken's parents to listen to the *Lux Radio Theater* on Sunday nights. Even Grandma could be found listening to her daily soap opera. *Ma Perkins* was sponsored by Oxydol Laundry Soap. Grandma always kept the bright orange and white box of soap handy on the shelf next to her wash tub and scrub board. It sat right next to her home-made lye soap that she used on extra dirty overalls and grimy hands, of course.

The short wave frequency remained a mysterious section of the radio dial. When Kenny's dad or grandpa turned that dial, strange howling sounds came from the radio. A little fine tuning brought in the static-interrupted voice of Edward R. Murrow from London or Hitler's boisterous voice from Germany.

When Hitler spoke, Ken couldn't understand him, but his dad and grandpa could. Once Hitler finished shouting, and the crowds answered him with their "Zig Heil" chant, Ken's dad and grandpa always broke into a heated argument about the speech they had just heard. Ken found out years later that his grandpa regarded Hitler as a hero for bringing Germany out of the Great Depression after the First World War. Unfortunately, his grandpa died in 1942 before he found out how wrong he was about his hero. On the other hand, Ken's father's prediction proved true, when Hitler turned out to be one of the greatest monsters the world would ever know.

Living under the same roof and sharing family stories over the supper table gave young Ken much practice in keeping his audience entertained with rich, innovative tales. Over the years, many people have assumed his varied adventures were only inventions of a fertile mind. Were they wrong? Judge for yourself . . .

Contents

Introduction 3

Part One: Where the Adventures Began

Wheels for Wings 15
Remembering Norfolk 24
How to grow chest hair in the Midwest 26
Robin Hood & the Widow's Chicken 32
Onaway from a Crash 38
Down in the Fox Holes 43

Part Two: Living to Tell About It

Scorched Debate Partner 55
Invention of the '42 Motor Home 59
White Dog Falls 66
Learning to Ski 71
Charlie Radford gets Married 74
The Gatorbait Adventures 80
The Exploding Mailbox 86
The Junior Mad Scientist 93
Getting into the House Moving Biz 100
Tri-Pacer Adventures 104
The Wine Cellar 110

Part Three: House Moving Adventures

Introducing John Jerks	117
Winch Truck on yo Sofa?	122
Canadian Washboard Fishing Trip	128
Turning Point in the Rotary Club	135
Two Story Monstrosity	138
Barn Shocker	141
Here Kitty Kitty	146
Bolts & Bulldozers	153
Purple Haze of High School	158
Best Christmas Ever!	163
No Way Around It	172
Down in the Dumps	177
Earning Your Stripes	181
Invention of the '42 Motor Home	187
Prince Albert & the Rubber Life Raft	193
Joe Mashayda's Hospital Project	198
The Grave Digger	204
Mudd and the Canadian Stoolspawner	211
The First Amphibian	216
Susie's Story	223

Part Four: The Asphalt Business

Fire Up the Distributor Truck 233
Hinky Dinky & the White Convertible 236
Swift Packing Company 238
2,000 lb Rubber Ducks 240
Taking the Long Shot 247
Drunken Davenport Mechanic 254
Papa Smurf 260
The Skunk Sweater 263
Lark 5 Amphibian 266
Jet Fuel & Avgas 269
Hot Oil Heaters 274
The Plant Gate 276
Waking the Dead in Barstow, CA 279
A Sweet Helicopter Deal 282

Acknowledgements 297

Part One

Where the Adventures Began

Wheels for Wings

1951

By Ken's junior year he was occasionally allowed to drive his father's 1950 blue four-door Ford to school while his father took the '48 Buick to work every day. During a conversation at the supper table one evening, Ken's father discovered his son was doing more than just driving at sixteen.

While Ken's grandmother gathered up the last of the supper dishes, his mother placed a home baked peach pie and a bowl of fresh whipping cream in the middle of the table.

"What did you do today, Kenny?" Mr. Bauer asked his son.

Mrs. Bauer cut into the pie and large flakey crumbs fell to the linen table cloth. "We had a half day at school, and I just had this terrible urge to go out to the airport, so I went for a drive out to Council Bluffs."

"What in the world did you go out there for?" Dad asked.

"You know how much I love model airplanes?"

"Uh huh," his father answered.

"I wanted to go look at the airplanes, and, well," Ken snatched up a piece of pie crust from the table cloth and popped it into his mouth, "and I bought an airplane."

"You what?" his father asked through a mouthful of pie.

"I bought an airplane."

"Oh, well does it have a nice wing span?" Mr. Bauer asked, thinking he'd picked up a model.

"Yeah, I think it's about 30 feet."

"Thirty feet?!!" his father exclaimed.

"Yeah," Ken told his father, "it's a real airplane."

"Come on? How could you buy a real airplane?"

"I paid $5 down on it."

"Nobody would sell a kid an airplane for $5 down."

"Oh, yes they would!" Ken insisted.

"So how much is the entire airplane going to end up costing you, Kenneth?"

"$595. It's a 1946 Aeronca 7AC Champ. It's yellow with a red curved stripe on the bottom; a beautiful airplane - just beautiful, Dad!" Ken leaned back in his chair to share his afternoon with his father.

"Do you remember Harry McCandlesss?" His father shook his head. "Well, he is a real character." Ken chuckled, thinking back to his afternoon with Harry. "When I got there this guy came out of the office and introduced himself and I told him my name. Then he asked me if I was related to Wayne – "

"Son - forget about your brother, what about the plane?" His father was intrigued.

"Oh, yeah – well, then he says, 'I'll be damned, meeting Wayne's little brother out here . . . how 'bout that! Say, have you got an airplane yet, Ken?' and I told him no, I haven't got one yet."

Mr. Bauer's head shook in disbelief as his son continued his story.

"Then he says to me, 'Ken - you outta by this one!'

"I should? I said to him. And we're standing there looking at the plane. And you know what, Dad . . .?"

"No. What?"

"I couldn't think of a single reason why I shouldn't have a plane."

"Except maybe you don't have any money?"

"Sure, except for that." Ken agreed.

"But it gets better, Dad. Harry says to me, 'Yeah, This is a hell of an airplane. You see this fabric on here? It's just like your model airplanes. You just put a bed sheet on here and put dope on there and fix any hole!"

"Yeah? What else did he tell you?"

"He unbuttoned the cowl and pointed up inside and he says to me, 'You see this engine here — this is exactly the same as a lawn mower – only it has 3 more cylinders! If anything went wrong – why you could fix it!'

"But the best part was when he asked me, 'How 'bout it? – you want to go up and try 'er out?' I didn't know what to say to him!"

"Let me guess . . ." Mr. Bauer took a drink of his coffee.

"Well, I tried to get out of it, Dad. I told Harry I haven't got any money. He told me that it was alright because he knew my brother. 'Let's go up' he says to me."

"You went flying?"

"Yes!" Ken said.

"Once we're up in the plane, Harry says to me, 'You see that stick there between your legs - if you push that forward, it goes down.' So I try it." Ken mimics the experience for his father. "I push it forward and by God, sure enough – it went down! Then he says to me, 'if you pull it back, it'll go up.' I pull it back, and sure enough - it went up."

"You were flying this plane, Kenny?"

"Yeah, it's easier than I would have ever thought, Dad!"

"By yourself?"

"Sure." Ken said. "I mean, he was right there behind me the whole time. But I was flying! He showed me how if you move the stick to the left, it will bank to left –if you move it to the right, it will bank right. . ."

Ken propped his heels on the kitchen linoleum for another demonstration. "Harry pointed down to the pedals on the floor and says to me, 'now those are rudder pedals. When you want to turn a corner, you just push on that pedal in whatever direction you want to turn and you can bank the airplane a little bit and you'll go right on around a corner.' So I tried it, and we did!"

His father was grinning now, imagining his son's experience.

"After we made a few turns Harry says to me, "I'll be damned – I've never seen anybody learn to fly as quickly as you did. This is amazing. I suppose knowing who your brother is, it makes sense."

Mr. Bauer nodded proudly at his young son.

Ken was proud as well. "I kept thinking 'MY GOD, I never dreamed I'd learn to fly an airplane in less than half an hour!"

"You must be a natural." His father offered. "Don't tell me that you landed this airplane?"

"No, no. When we got ready to go back, Harry says, 'I'd let ya land 'er – but you probably ought to have another lesson before we do that." Father and son shared a quiet laugh.

"So we landed," Ken continued with his story, "and Harry says, 'So you wanna buy 'er?' I said to Harry, 'I can't. I haven't got any money.' But he isn't convinced. He says, 'Surely you got some money?' and I tell him that all I have is my allowance and I reach in my pocket."

"How much did you have on you?"

"My whole weeks allowance. I pulled out a five dollar bill."

Mr. Bauer smiled. "What did he have to say about that?"

"He says, 'I'll tell ya what, I'll take $5 down and we'll figure out some way to finance 'er.'"

"Are you kidding me?"

"Nope. I looked right at Harry and I said, 'Ok' and I handed him the $5."

"He took $5 down on an airplane?"

"Yup." Ken answered proudly.

"What a day you had son."

"I sure did, Dad. Anyhow," Ken stood up from the dinner table, "tomorrow is Saturday. Tell you what, Dad – why don't we go out there together and I'll show you my airplane."

The next morning Ken and his father arrived at the airport. Harry rushed out of the office the moment he saw Ken. Ken introduced his father to the smooth talking airplane salesman.

"Are you Wayne Bauer's father?" Harry said offering a firm handshake to Mr. Bauer. "I went to school with Wayne. Man, I have been looking forward to meeting you!"

"Nice to meet you, Harry." Mr. Bauer said, returning the greeting. "So, Ken's been telling me a tall tale about $5's down on an airplane."

"That's right. It was $5 down, it wasn't for the whole airplane." Harry tells him and both men chuckle.

Joe Bauer opened his mouth to speak, but Harry quickly interrupted. "That kid of yours – he's amazing – he can fly. Never in my life have I seen someone fly in such a short period like he can – you must have that in your blood!"

Joe didn't know what to say.

"Mr. Bauer, why don't you come up with me," he said, extending an arm toward the plane, while placing the other arm around Mr. Bauer's shoulders, "I want *you* to see how she flies." With nothing to lose, Joe agreed and the two men walk toward the plane. Ken watched Harry take his father up into the air.

Once Ken's father was back on the ground he told his son, "By God, I could fly that airplane. I couldn't believe it! We can both fly!" Ken smiled at his father; they were equally proud of one another.

Monday morning Mr. Bauer made a trip to his Credit Union and borrowed $590; the difference between the $5 Ken had given Harry for the down payment and the price of the airplane.

Ken and his father were the proud owners of a 1946 Aeronca 7AC Champ.

* * *

Harry McCandless flew Ken's new airplane from the Council Bluffs airport to Clear Ridge airport, located 3 miles from Ken's home. A flight instructor by the name of Andy Anderson became Ken's new best friend at $5 an hour.

Andy explained how the FAA required at least eight hours of dual flying time before he could solo and at least 40 hours total before he could take the check ride for his license.

Ken wasted no time; his first one hour flying lesson took place the very next day. Andy turned out to be a demanding coach, so when Ken walked up to his new plane feeling ten feet tall and bullet-proof he received quite the wake-up call. Turns out he really wasn't the hot-shot pilot Harry McCandless made him out to be up in the clear blue yonder.

His instructor expected perfection from every maneuver. They started out with simple turns, progressed to more complex maneuvers like dives and stalls, and eventually worked on landings; which were to be perfect three point touch downs.

Early in the training this meticulous pilot insisted on teaching Ken emergency landing procedures. He would either "chop the throttle" to idle or shut off the engine completely, forcing Ken to land. These landing practices gave Ken the confidence to land in fields rather than airports.

Ken was required to quickly locate a field big enough to land in and close enough where the airplane could glide to a touchdown without using any power. Andy was famous for his element of surprise, usually during some complicated maneuver.

Andy also taught Ken how to "prop" the airplane, especially because Ken's plane was primitive by today's standards; no electrical system, no lights, no radio, not even an engine starter.

"Propping" the engine required two people: one on the ground, and another person inside the cockpit. The person in the cockpit was responsible for controlling the throttle and ignition switch and more importantly, holding the brakes.

Meanwhile, the person on the ground had to place their hands flat on the left blade of the propeller, then balance on the left foot while swinging the right foot backwards to give the body and arms the momentum to spin the prop. This started the engine. However, the "proper" must be mindful to avoid getting any body parts caught in the prop when once the engine started!

The day finally came when Andy felt confident for Ken to fly solo. Of course he didn't tell Ken ahead of time, however Ken's suspicion was confirmed when his instructor insisted he strap on a seat pack parachute.

The whole time they were in the air, Ken couldn't help but think about the stories he'd heard around the airport from the other students. Apparently, Andy had once been a barn stormer and was comfortable bailing out of airplanes on a moment's notice. Rumor had it that during one of his student's solo flights, he opened the door and dropped out of the plane in mid-flight! It was difficult for Ken to concentrate on his performance because he kept looking back at his instructor, wondering when he was going to disappear on him.

Ultimately, Andy stayed in the plane while Ken performed a couple of takeoffs, completed a few landings, and on the last landing Andy got out of the plane. Ken took flight by himself.

He was scared to death but after several passes around the field an incredible sense of pride overwhelmed him. He managed perfect takeoffs and landings. Moreover, during his solo flight he realized what kind of freedom this meant for him; he could fly where ever he wanted, perform the maneuvers he chose, and he was capable of landing nearly anywhere on earth, under *any* circumstances - all thanks to Andy.

Ken finalized all of the required hours, passed his FAA written exam, and completed the FAA check ride in the airplane, passing all with flying colors! Now, as a licensed private pilot with the rating of 'private pilot, airplane, single-engine land' he felt his life started that very day.

It was time for the adventures to begin!

Remembering Norfolk

1952

Immediately after Ken received his private pilot's license he joined the Civil Air Patrol as a volunteer pilot. The CAP helped with search and rescue operations and other missions approved by the officers.

Ken's first assignment was to help test the Ground Observer Corp. This volunteer organization was carried over from WWII and they were responsible for reporting enemy air craft.

The concept was simple: The CAP planes were to fly at an altitude of 500 feet in a formation of three. The mission started in Norfolk, Nebraska, where they flew over designated areas assigned to the observers stationed on the ground. The observers were to first identify the planes and then report how many flew overhead. Ken thought it would be romantic to take his high school sweetheart along on the mission.

"Do you think we should eat something?" Alice asked Ken as they walked through the Norfolk airport together.

"Not much is open." Ken looked around and spotted a snack bar. "How about a root-beer float?"

"At seven o'clock in the morning?" Alice wrinkled up her nose at Ken, but followed him up to the counter anyway.

The two clinked glasses and downed their breakfast before heading to Ken's airplane. The teenagers were soon airborne for the first half of the mission.

The predetermined flight turned out to be over 100 miles long. During the early morning hours the air was fairly smooth, but that changed as the ground beneath them began to warm over the course of the flight. Ken and Alice discovered that the multicolored farmland caused all sorts of up drafts and down drafts, making the flight incredibly choppy.

By the time they returned to Norfolk on the first route, Alice was feeling nauseated. Ken finished the second leg of the mission by himself.

After an hour into the flight the bouncing got to Ken as well. He decided it might be best to get out of the air for a few minutes. He picked out a field to land in that looked much like short alfalfa. Upon approach, Ken spotted a couple of nice haystacks.

Crawling down out of the cockpit he headed straight for the pile of golden hay where he could lie down and close his eyes for a while. Drifting off under the quiet, blue sky, Ken thought about his earlier approach to a field where he had flown over a farmhouse with a yard full of chickens.

Although he was miserable with the threat of vomiting, he managed a smile at the fat little hens he'd startled when he flew past in his airplane. This took him back to his many childhood adventures.

Ken nuzzled down into the coolness of the hay to ease his troubled stomach and dozed off to dream of chickens and chest hair.

How to grow chest hair in the Midwest

1939

Mr. Dreyer had a hairy chest. This fascinated young five year old Kenneth Bauer. The man frequently stood behind a short, weathered picket fence that desperately needed paint, while tending to a small garden and his many chickens.

Ken's best friend happened to live across the street from the large German man. It was from the comfort of Donnie's front yard that Ken would watch and wonder about the cultivated furry secret the man across the street was keeping from him.

Although Mr. Dreyer was only in his mid thirties, he seemed very old and wise to young Ken. One afternoon while the gardener tended his yard, Ken worked up enough nerve to stroll across the street and ask him about his hairy chest.

Reaching the other side of the Dreyer fence, Ken asked, "Mr. Dreyer," the man was busy turning over dark Nebraska soil with his hoe. "How do you get that chest hair to grow like that?"

Mr. Dreyer stopped what he was doing, stood up tall and turned to look down at Ken. "Well, son" he removed his hat and wiped his brow with a long sleeve from his flannel shirt, "is lot like growing potatoes or anything else. You have to fertilize."

"You do?" Ken questioned with curiosity. The little boy stared up at the giant, whose large straw hat partially blocked the sun in Ken's eyes. *This guy was a heck of a farmer*, Ken thought to himself, *he must know what he's talking about*. So he inquired further.

"What do you put on there?" he asked the wise, hairy farmer.

Mr. Dreyer leaned on the wooden handle of his hoe, "Well, don't tell anyone about dis, or you have to die, ya?" Kenny stared back with intense brown eyes while Mr. Dreyer continued to tease, "because dis is old secret where I come from." He said, pinching the corner of his mouth to conceal a growing smirk.

"Dis only grows hair," he pointed a long dirty finger at the boy. "Is not for da potatoes." He told Ken.

"Really? What is it? What is it?!" The young boy asked, eager to know his secret.

The German man continued, "You see da chicken shit there on da ground there? You see dat some of it in there is white," he kicked a bit of the chicken droppings around, "you see dat?" He looked over to see Ken thoroughly examining the excrement, "some of it's brown, some of it's green, ya? Now, da brown is good for da potatoes and da green is good for da tomatoes. But that white – see dat there," he was pointing, "now you put dat white on your chest and it makes da hair grow."

"*Reeeealy?*" Ken dropped to his knees to examine closely.

"Ya." Mr. Dreyer answered.

Oh my god, I gotta try this! Ken thought to himself. So he crawled around on his hands and knees there in Mr. Dreyer's chicken yard looking for piles of poo that had white flecks in it.

An amused Mr. Dreyer reminded him, "Be very careful just to get da white."

Young Kenneth obediently carried out his instructions, careful to avoid any of the green or the brown. Once he collected his little white pile, he asked Mr. Dreyer, "is this enough to rub on my chest?"

Mr. Dreyer smiled proudly, "Ya, ya, dat should do it."

* * *

Later that evening when Ken sat down at the dinner table, his mother's face scrunched up in disgust. She looked over at her young son.

"*What* is that smell?" she asked.

Proudly, young Ken sat up tall in his chair and answered, "That's my hair growing fertilizer."

"Your what?!" she asked. He watched her eyebrows slowly began to head north. From past experience, Ken knew this was not a good sign.

"Well," Ken began again, only this time a little less sure of himself, "I got some fertilizer that grows hair on my chest."

"My God!" Mother shot up out of her chair and circled to his side of the table. Then with lightening fast, alien-like tentacle arms she had a hold of his shirt.

"Lemme see it," she said, stretching the neck-hole of his yellow T-shirt down to see what he was talking about.

And there it was.

His mother hovered over him, her mouth held open in amazement (*a look Kenny was becoming oh-so familiar with*). Poor mother, unable to speak, stared at the white chicken shit spread all over her son's chest.

With one quick, frightened breath, Ken defended himself, "Mr. Dreyer told me that his hairy chest came from putting white chicken-poo on it."

His mothers frozen stance was interrupted only by his father's instantaneous fury.

"I can't believe he'd do that. I'm going go down there and kick his ass!" Joe shouted. Luckily, mother quickly came to her senses and leveler heads prevailed.

"No, no," she gently offered, "*this*, we can clean up."

And she did, hauling her chicken-poo covered child off to the bathtub where she scrubbed him from head, to dirty little toe with a terrycloth washrag. Mother turned Ken's chest a candy-apple red, instead of the dark-furry brown, as he had hoped.

However, this did not discourage young Kenneth. Underneath his bald little chest, deep in his great big confident heart, he knew that his parents could not possibly understand the highly secret things that Mr. Dreyer had shared with him. And so for the next several weeks, convinced that the fertilizer had time enough to do some good, he carefully inspected his chest for signs of fertilized chest hair.

* * *

Ken awoke on the haystack, the smile still on his face, having returned to childhood over a short nap. The nausea had subsided and he stretched his arms overhead, rolled over to his knees, and stood up to walk back to his airplane -

only to face another challenge on his Norfolk Civil Air Patrol mission.

Starting his engine was a two-person operation and he realized what a terrible mistake he'd made shutting off the engine. Ken had to devise a way to keep the plane in place while propping it by himself.

He looked around the field to find something to wedge under the wheels. The only things available were a handful of old rotten corn stalks. Ken wedged them under the wheels, and attempted to start the engine by opening the throttle in small increments. These attempts failed.

Knowing he must open it further to get the engine to start, Ken discovered another mistake. He cracked the throttle open further than necessary, propped the engine again, and the plane started. Only now, the airplane ran over the stalks and charged straight at its pilot!

Luckily he was able to dive away from the spinning propeller without losing any of his parts. He quickly realized the airplane was going to get away from him if he didn't grab hold of the wing strut when the plane growled past. Running as fast as his feet could carry him, Ken managed to open the airplane door and leap inside.

Once airborne he dropped down low, flying back over the chicken coop scattering the black and white speckled hens in every which direction. On his ascent back into the blue vastness he dodged several billowy clouds only to have his stomach protest again.

Forcing a few deep breaths, Ken thought of Mr. Dreyer. Focusing on something other than the airsickness, he visualized the picket fence of his childhood. He remembered the Dreyer corn fields where he used to play Robin Hood with his bow and arrow. Ken could still see the look on the old farmer's face the day he showed up with a chicken in hand, skewered with one of his arrows.

Robin Hood & the Widow's Chicken

1943

Uhh-oh, Kenny thought when he heard Mr. Dreyer's voice at the front door on a Saturday morning. From a safe distance in the kitchen, the nine year old watched his dad visit with the neighbor.

"Joe," the angry neighbor asked Mr. Bauer, holding up a chicken impaled with an arrow through its midsection, "do you know anything about this?"

* * *

Like many youngsters in the 1940s, Ken was largely influenced by the movies. He happened to be particularly enthralled with Robin Hood and the fact that he was a marksman with a bow and arrow. Naturally, the young enthusiast thought to himself, *how tough could it be?*

Ken asked his folks to buy him a bow and arrow, which they did. The Bauer's, being responsible parents to their spirited son, purchased a bow with arrows that had rubber suction cups on the tips.

Come to find out, shooting arrows was a bit more difficult than he had hoped. Ken fastened a target to the back of the garage and began practicing.

At first, he missed the target entirely but eventually he got a few arrows to stick into the middle. Also, the bow string slapped against his arm with every release and it burned his skin like mad; so he double layered his long-sleeve shirts, pretending it was his protective armor. After several days of practice it was time to modify his equipment.

The suction cups did not set well with Ken. He fully realized that Robin Hood would never shoot arrows with rubber tips on them! So he removed them. He took his arrows to a pencil sharpener and round and round he turned the pencil sharpener until he had nice, sharp points on each one.

"Now we got something going!" he said to himself.

Armed with his bow and arrows, Ken set off to - *well*, Ken wondered, *what exactly did Robin Hood do all day*? After careful consideration he realized that when Robin Hood was out hunting, he robbed from the rich and gave to the poor. So that was a good place to start.

Ken's new adventure led him out to the Dreyer cornfield. Mr. Dreyer had a whole bunch of chickens that ran around in his corn patch. So many, in fact, that Ken decided it was more chickens than any one man needed.

So for several hours he snuck up and down the corn rows pretending he was in Sherwood Forest. Upon spotting one of Mr. Dreyer's chickens, he would aim, shoot, and miss.

"Those darn chickens are fast." Ken said under his breath. Much like the target on the garage, his persistence and practice paid off. His aim got better and he hit one of the chickens. But to his surprise, she ran off with his arrow! This was much tougher than he expected.

Finally he got one – dead center and dead instantly! Wow! That felt great! *Now what would Robin Hood do with this chicken*? Ken wondered.

The first person who came to mind was Josie, the cute little blond haired, blue-eyed girl who lived in Ken's neighborhood. Her dad had died, leaving her, her sister and brother, alone with their mother.

Ken and Josie were the same age and they played together, so he knew they didn't have much money and their mother had fallen on really hard times. Robin Hood would certainly approve of his choice to help Josie and her mom. Ken headed for Josie's; proud in the fact that he had done robbed from rich ol' Mr. Dreyer to give to the poor widow.

When young Robin Hood arrived at their home, Josie's mother had finished washing the neighbor's clothes and she was about to iron them. He walked up to the back porch where he could see them in the kitchen with the ironing board and he knocked on the door.

"Hello Kenneth" Josie's mom greeted him. "Come on in." Ken opened the screen door, walked in, and without hesitation he held the chicken proudly over his head to the widow. Her eyes widened in surprise at the chicken with an arrow sticking through the middle.

"Whatcha got there, kiddo?" She asked Ken and he wasn't sure how to explain, so he just smiled. And to his surprise, she absolutely loved it! "Why, isn't that – wonderful!" She said, staring at the arrow-skewered-chicken.

Once Josie's mom accepted the fowl, Ken convinced himself he would have everyone fooled!

Just like Robin Hood, no one will ever know where that chicken came from. Of course the sweet little widow certainly wasn't about to look this gift horse in the mouth, so she plucked her chicken and put it in a pot for their Friday night dinner.

Ken floated home. The benevolent act he had performed left him feeling ten feet tall. This glorious feeling lasted right up until Mr. Dreyer knocked on his front door the next morning.

*　*　*

"Kenny, come here." His father calmly commanded. "What do you know about this?"

Ken flipped the rolodex back in his mind, remembering his chicken killing spree. *Oh shoot! The one that got away!*

Ken realized it must be that speared chicken that took off with his arrow. Ol' Mr. Dreyer must have gone out there and found that chicken - dead with an arrow through him. *Boy was he smart to know where to look for the culprit*, Ken decided.

It turned out that Mr. Dreyer had a ramp that lead all the way up to his chicken house. That damned chicken headed home after she'd been shot and tried to make it up the ramp and into the chicken house. But, at the end of the ramp there's a hole that the chickens have to run through.

"Dis chicken here," he dangled the dead bird in mid air, "she not make it true da hole because she got da arrow true her!"

"Well, Kenny?" Mr. Bauer turned to his son. Ken could see the whole thing now. He shook his head in disgust at the stupid chicken. "No? You don't know anything about this?" His father asked again, misinterpreting the head shake.

"No. Well, I mean, yes," he looked up at the two angry men, "yes, I think I know what happened."

"Would you like to explain what happened to me and Mr. Dreyer, please?"

"Well Dad," he began, "I was trying to help Josie's mother, just like Robin Hood."

The two men exchanged a quick glance. Mr. Dreyer took off his hat to scratch his head, while Mr. Bauer knelt down to talk with his son.

"Do you remember what happened to Robin Hood when the sheriff caught him?"

His young son looked down at his bare feet and thought for moment. "Uhm, he took him to jail?" He offered to his father; much like the uncertainty of answering one of his school teachers.

"That's right," he confirmed, "and that is exactly what is going to happen to you. I'm also going to burn that damn bow and all of your arrows."

"I've only got one left," Ken said, "Mr. Dreyer probably has all the others in his chickens." From the look in his father's eyes, Ken calculated that was information he probably should have kept to himself.

"To your room young man," father pointed over his head as he stood to tower above his son, "and I don't want to see you until supper time."

A disappointed Ken shuffled down the hallway to his room. Alone in his shame, he sulked. But it didn't take long to cheer himself up again. *I will plan a jail break*, he thought . . . *because that's what Robin Hood would do*!

* * *

After a trip down memory Ken's mind was back on flying his airplane. The rest had alleviated some of the airsickness; Ken had several miles yet to fly until he reached Norfolk. His stomach continued to claw away at his insides until he was scrambling to open a window; he was too late.

The root beer float came up and spewed all over the inside of the airplane, covering the instrument panel and his lap. Ken discovered several things that afternoon on his return flight.

He realized that a root-beer breakfast is a bad idea, that a Norfolk mission is not romantic, and perhaps he should bring someone along to assist him in starting his airplane to avoid any further potential death-by-propeller episodes.

Onaway from a Crash

1952

Fifteen year old Donnie Wilson awoke on the Fourth of July to find that he was home alone. His folks were on their way to the annual family picnic at his uncle's farm, a hundred miles away, and Donnie had to figure out how to get there.

After pulling on a pair of Levi's he stumbled to the medicine cabinet, and popped a couple of aspirin into his mouth. He bent over to the faucet for a mouthful of water to help swallow the chalky little pills. In the living room he slumped down into his dad's recliner, and feeling the cool leather against his bare skin, he dialed Ken's number.

"Hey Ken," Donnie was grateful that Ken picked up so he didn't have to speak to Mr. or Mrs. Bauer, "could you do me a favor?"

Donnie explained that his parents had left him home sleeping because he'd been out late the night before. He asked Ken to fly him to his uncle's Fourth of July picnic near Onawa, Iowa.

"Sure. Sounds like fun." Ken laughed through a mouthful of eggs while he ate his breakfast at the kitchen counter and talked on the telephone. They agreed to meet at Clear Ridge airport within the hour.

Once the boys met up at the airport they went through the preflight check and the engine starting procedures. Donnie climbed into the cockpit and Ken propped the engine.

After they were airborne, Ken shouted over the loud engine noise: "Do you want me to land at the Onawa airport?"

"I was kinda hoping we didn't have to go to an airport; that maybe you could just fly right into my uncle's farm?" Donnie shouted back.

"Sure." Ken replied, thinking to himself - *how hard could that be?*

The boys flew the hundred miles from Clear Ridge airport to the uncle's farm.

Donnie said to Ken, "I think you take this road here," he pointed through the windshield, "no, follow that other road there…"

Ken flew low level down the roads Donnie selected.

"Ok," Donnie instructed, "now turn left here. Over there," he was pointing to a two-story red barn in back of a house with a white picket fenced stitched around the property line. "That's it – right there! See all those cars parked over there? They've already started the picnic." Donnie was excited that he'd located his uncles' property from the air.

"Alright." Ken acknowledged. "Where do you think I could land?"

"There's an alfalfa field out in back of the barn. You could land out there."

Ken nodded. He noticed that the field out behind the barn was green. So he circled around, flew low level over it again to take another look. It didn't really look like alfalfa, but whatever was growing there appeared to be green and short; or so Ken thought.

He circled the field and came back over the fence, chopped the throttle, and dropped into a crop of young, wet wheat about 3 feet high that put so much drag on the wheels that the airplane stopped almost immediately.

Taxiing up to the farm house turned out to be a bit of a challenge. As Ken cut a swath through the wheat, the propeller chopped it into a green slurry and blew it onto the windshield. Since Donnie roughly knew where the house was, he successfully guided Ken to the back yard.

As it was, the boys made it to the farmhouse and surprisingly no one was upset about the wheat field. The Fourth of July picnic was an absolute treat. However, once it was time to go home, more trouble awaited Ken and his airplane.

His first challenge was dodging the fences that he couldn't see through his green windshield. Ken made several attempts before realizing the wheat on the wheels and struts created so much drag that the airplane wouldn't fly.

"Well, that didn't work." He told Donnie after a few failed attempts. "We need to get some weight out of here – why don't you climb out and go up to the road. I'll get out of this field and land out on the road and pick you up."

"Ok." Donnie unbuckled and hopped out of the airplane.

Ken tried one more time to pick a spot that he had already cut down. With less weight, he knew the only way to become airborne was to bounce the front wheels off the ground several times in order to clear the wheat. With a few hops, he was in the air!

Flying over the road where Donnie had been instructed to wait, Ken realized that he should have examined the road before deciding to land there.

With his windshield painted green, Ken looked out the side window and noticed power lines down one side of the road and telephone lines down the other. Both had cross arms at different heights turning this landing strip into a potential obstacle course. He was going to have to figure out a way to bank the airplane, fit his wings between those cross arms, and land on the road. Ken circled around and prepared for his landing to pick up Donnie.

"I can do this," he said under his breath.

He banked to the right and got his first wing in under the power line cross arm, then quickly banked the aircraft to the left to successfully get under the telephone line cross arm.

A moment of pride washed over Ken in the cockpit, realizing he had negotiated this obstacle course. However, seconds later, just before touching down, Ken's left wing slammed into a hedge tree and spun the plane around, crashing him into a ditch. Donnie immediately ran toward Ken and the crash site, along with several people from the picnic.

"Are you hurt?" A lady with a floppy yellow sun-hat asked Ken.

"No." Ken told her. "But I think I broke my airplane, though." The large crowd gathering was going to be a bigger problem than the crash.

"We've got to get this plane out of here." Ken said to Donnie. "Landing on roads is illegal."

"How about crashing on them, is that illegal too?" Donnie tried to lighten the mood.

"The last thing I need is the county Sherriff out here asking me questions."

"Maybe you'd rather try explaining what you did to the FAA?" Donnie's uncle teased.

"Yeeahh, right!" Ken smiled back at the two of them.

Donnie's uncle fired up his tractor and attached a logging chain. They hooked on to the tail of the plane sticking out of the ditch and drug the broken plane into his yard. They rested the sorrowful looking thing under a tree and Ken stood back to look at the damage.

The propeller was broken and there was a large hole in the bottom of the fuselage where he must have hit the edge of the ditch. The wing strut on the left side was bent, the left wing was bent back a foot, and the air foil was caved in about two feet from the wing tip. There was nothing more that could be done today. The boys left the plane at the farm and rode home with Donnie's parents.

"You boys are unbelievable!" Donnie's mother lectured over her shoulder from the front seat. The two of them spent the next several miles listening to her recount all of the trouble they had managed to get themselves into over the years.

"No, no" Andrew disagreed at one point, "the worst was when you boys dug that big hole in my garden. What did you call it? A foxhole?" He asked, looking into the rearview mirror.

"It was a cave" Donnie answered.

"No, it was a tunnel." Ken said and the boys quickly shared a wily grin with each other.

"What ever you called it - that was the worst thing that ever happened to my garden." It was clear that Andrew still hadn't gotten over that shenanigan and that was almost six years ago!

Down in the Fox Holes

1946

Ken and Donnie loved going to the movies and some of their favorites were the war films.

Quite often, the two twelve year olds could be found submersing their hands into a bucket of buttery popcorn, not taking their eyes off of the ten foot tall prisoners on the big screen.

The black and white characters of *Stalag 17* were imprisoned in a war camp. They were concealing their prison break by digging their way out and carrying the dirt in their pants with drawstrings on the bottoms of them. They would release the strings and let the dirt fallout as they walked around the prison yard.

This was most impressive to the boys, because it was a plan devised so that no one could discover what they were up to; a concept these two were familiar with and appreciated greatly.

Walking home in the warm night air, Ken and Donnie talked about the tunnels that the prisoners dug.

"We could dig a tunnel just like in the movie!" Ken said. "We could dig underground rooms connected by tunnels. It would be the best hide out ever!"

The next morning, in their excitement, they devised a plan to begin digging their tunnels in Donnie's fathers' field. Both boys fantasized that it would be just like in the movie; no one would ever know what they were up to! And they would do like the prisoners and carefully distribute their diggings so there were no large mounds of dirt to give them away . . . *how tough could it be?*

The first hardship they ran into was how to hide the different colors of dirt. As the boys dug deeper into the ground, the color of the dirt changed. They found themselves trying to mix the yellow-clay like soil in with Andrew's rich black top soil to hide their work.

While finishing up their dirt distribution that day, they agreed it was important to figure out a way to cover the entrance to their underground world.

"We don't want anyone finding out about our secret fort." Donnie reminded Ken.

"Well, let's look around here and see what we can use."

They found a large wooden spool that once had wire wrapped around it and now it was missing an end. So they stuffed the core of the spool down into the opening of the hole so that the flat, round end covered flush to the ground. They kicked dirt and loose foliage over the top to cover and camouflage their secret entrance.

After days of digging they started to dig sideways and dug out their first room. The boys agreed that they needed another. So several days later, they had finished digging their second room.

While appreciating all of their hard work, Ken came up with a thought. "Now maybe we could even get Josie to come down here!" It seemed the boys were trying to get their little neighborhood girl friend to join them more often these days.

The days of digging their fort had flown by and soon their summer break was over. Even after returning to school, the young boys enjoyed their fort.

"We need some lights down in here." Donnie said sitting next to Ken in the secret cave.

"You're right." Ken agreed. "I got an idea, Donnie. Let's collect a bunch of those pint milk cartons from school," he suggested. "If we cut the tops off, and a window in one side, and put a candle down in them, that would make great lights for our hide-out."

"Oh ya, Ken, that's a great idea!"

Once they had their lights designed, they returned to the dirt fort, climbed down inside and dug little shelves into the walls where they could place their candles. Pleased with their work they both stood back to admire their soft, candle-lit accomplishments.

"I think Josie would really like it down here now." Ken said to Donnie.

"Yup. I'll bet she would."

The boys worked on their hideout late into the fall. With winter coming, they would have to retire the project until next spring. Besides, there would be other things to occupy their time once the snow fell. And that is exactly what happened; the boys got busy doing other things and forgot about their fort.

* * *

The following spring, during a warm afternoon as they walked home from school, they noticed something out of place on their familiar neighborhood street.

"Donnie, look over there." Ken pointed to Andrew's field.

"It looks like a tow truck is lifting that horse!" Donnie exclaimed.

"I can't believe it . . ." Ken said. The two boys looked at each other and quickly headed toward the scene.

They didn't have to get much closer to see Andrew's red face and flailing arms. Boy was he mad! And so was his friend Ernie Dunton who had brought his horse over to plow the field.

What had taken place (just a few hours earlier while the boys busied themselves with their arithmetic problems) was that horse had begun to plow Andrew's garden, but his weight was too much for the hollowed out rooms the boys had built.

While Dunton and his horse trod over the secret hideout, the whole damn thing caved in and the horse had gotten stuck down in the boys' hole! The boys stared in awe at the bug-eyed, whinnying, horse kicking in mid air while he dangled from the end of the winch line!

Andrew was shouting apologies to his friend over the growl and whine of the tow truck while he looked down into the enormous hole that he had no way of refilling.

The boys had done such an efficient job at spreading the dirt evenly across the property that the whole field would need to be scraped to gather the necessary dirt. Without Dunton's help it would take Andrew an entire week to accomplish.

"Once I get my horse outta this damn hole," Dunton was shouting back, "I don't want to have anything more to do with this mess."

Andrew handed a check over to the tow truck driver, reached for his son's arm and headed for home. The last thing Ken noticed was Andrew's wide, blazing eyeballs.

A large lump grew in Ken's throat with each step he took toward his house. He was certain that either his Grandmother or his parents, or all of them, had received the news by now.

Operation foxhole had gone terribly wrong and Ken knew that both he and Donnie were the ones about to be imprisoned for a very, very, long time.

* * *

It seemed that Donnie's folks were right. Not much had changed for Ken and Donnie in the past six years, as the two continued to get into trouble together. Ken thanked Donnie's folks for the ride home.

The next morning, Ken borrowed his dad's Ford and drove to Clear Ridge airport where his friend Rolly Nelson worked as an FAA certified mechanic.

"Rolly," Ken asked the mechanic, watching him work on the underbelly of an airplane, "*theoretically* – if a guy would happen to land on a road and he'd happen to damage the plane, what would the FAA have to say about it?"

"Well," Rolly grunted tightening a rivet, "*theoretically*, does this guy like his license?"

"Oh, yeah, he does."

"Well," he said wiping his hands on a greasy red rag, "we don't mention things like that to the FAA." He looked over at Ken. "How much damage to the airplane?"

"I don't know."

"If you can fix it for less than $200, you don't have to report it to the FAA."

Ken knew what he needed to do.

Purchasing a used wing strut and an old wooden propeller he went home to swipe one of his mother's bed sheets and found his model airplane dope. Now he and Donnie could go fix his airplane.

The following weekend the boys drove Mr. Bauer's Ford back out to the farm where his plane was laid up. Looking over the airplane, Ken wondered if he could fix the damage. And even if he could – would it fly?

"What all do we have to replace?" Donnie asked Ken as they stared at the crashed heap.

"Replace? It needs to be replaced with a new airplane, is what it needs." Ken replied, realizing it should be repaired by an FAA licensed mechanic.

Fixing the damage wasn't going to be easy, as a matter of fact, it was going to take a lot of jerry-rigging because they didn't have the tools or knowledge to follow FAA procedures.

The first thing the young aviator and his assistant did was change the prop. This involved a ring of bolts around the center that had to be tightened so that the new propeller would track correctly.

Next, they cut the bed sheet, the size of the hole in the fuselage, and cemented it into place with model airplane dope. But the structure under the fuselage was also broken, leaving a big hollow spot in the center of their patch. Ken hoped this would not affect the flight characteristics of the aircraft.

The wing was going to be their biggest challenge.

"It looks pretty torn up, Ken."

"Yeah, but I think we can fix it."

Ken's concerns were two-fold. First, could he bend the wing back far enough to install a new strut, without cracking or breaking the aluminum wing connection points? Secondly, would the plane fly with the leading edge of the wing smashed flat about two feet in from the tip?

The teenage mechanics got busy and replaced the bent strut with a new one. The strut went on fine, the fastening points didn't seem to break or crack. He worried though, if there were an invisible crack, the fastener would break through and the wing might fall off in flight.

Ken shook the wing and hoped that it would stay put. They spent the morning band-aiding the plane as best they could.

Donnie's uncle towed the limping plane to an alfalfa field a half mile down the road. He unhitched the plane and dubiously wished Ken good luck. After Donnie assisted Ken in getting the plane started, he drove the Ford back to meet Ken at Clear Ridge airport.

Ken revved the engine up to maximum RPMs, released the brakes, and began his take off roll. The plane didn't want to lift up out of the field and he had a fence at the end he would have to clear.

He got the plane bouncing through the alfalfa, lifting higher off the ground with each bounce, until he cleared the fence. Now the problem was that the plane wouldn't climb – it just wanted to fly at the same altitude.

Fighting the control stick, he held it hard to the right just to keep the wings level. *It's got to be that flat airfoil*, he thought to himself, *it probably doesn't have any lift out there.*

Having to hold the stick hard right was killing the aerodynamics of the aircraft. Ken realized it was going to be impossible to make a right turn and he had to figure out a way to gain altitude because Clear Ridge sits about 1,200 feet above sea level.

Ken opted to fly low over the Missouri river, which is around 1,000 feet above sea level. This way he would avoid the hills and the trees. He figured that he would simply fly up the river toward Clear Ridge until he had another thought.

How am I going to get to Clear Ridge from the river, he worried, *I'm going to need another 200 feet in altitude . . .*

While contemplating this dilemma he flew over a creek. This appeared to him like the finger of God, it was pointing in the direction of Clear Ridge Airport!

Ken breathed a sigh of relief, deciding to follow the creek bed towards Clear Ridge and hopefully be able to gain the last 200 feet to make it up to the runway.

Following the twists and turns of the creek he noticed that every time he turned to the left the airplane climbed a little higher. Had he only discovered this while flying over the river, he could have probably circled to the left and gained the necessary altitude.

But now, coming to the end of the creek he realized what a risky situation he'd gotten himself. The valley he was flying through was too narrow to turn around. Climbing over the ridge in front of him was going to be a matter of do or die.

Arriving at the end of the creek he banked the plane to the left giving him just enough oomph to climb one last time. By lowering the aileron on the right wing he increased his lift and barely made it over the ridge and on to the runway.

Ken released his white knuckles from the stick after landing the airplane. He taxied back to the tie downs while counting his blessings; recognizing how fortunate he was to be alive. It wasn't long before his gratitude turned to excitement thinking of sharing his adventure with Donnie once he arrived to pick him up.

Ken taxied his broken airplane and thought of his folks, his friends, and his sweetheart Alice. He realized that he was one lucky young man.

Part Two

Living to Tell About It

Scorched Debate Partner

1951

Ken continued to excel in high school both academically and socially. Interestingly enough, it was during a PTA open house at Tech high school early in his junior year that Ken's mother had taught him to look at girls in a different light.

As the two of them meandered from classroom to classroom, Ken introduced his mother to several friends, acquaintances, and teachers. Mrs. Bauer noticed that her son was smitten when introducing one of the cute little cheerleaders, but she said nothing to embarrass him.

Ken saw Alice Parker coming down the hallway to chat with him and his mother. Mrs. Bauer took note of Alice's neatly groomed brown hair pulled back to showcase her piercing-blue eyes. She wore little make-up on her alabaster skin and she dressed in a conservative, neatly pressed fashion. Mrs. Bauer tapped her son on the shoulder.

"Now that is a nice, intelligent young lady, Kenny," she told her son. "It seems to me that if you're going to date somebody, you might prefer someone like that, rather than that flashy cheerleader." Although Ken had never given any thought to dating Alice to that point, he held his mother's opinion in high regard so he considered her suggestion and the two began seeing more of each other.

As for Mr. Bauer, Ken brought his father a tremendous amount of pride when he became one of the reigning champions on the high school debate team; a responsibility that provided Ken with a great sense of accomplishment. He also appreciated the fact that some of the most important people in his life were also part of the debate team: his sweetheart, Alice, and one of his closest friends, Clarence, who both shared the stage with him on a regular basis.

The boys shared a dovetailing interest: chemistry. Ken and Clarence played mad scientist every chance they got down in the Bauer basement, out in the garage, and in the high school chemistry lab. One day Clarence developed an explosive by combining two common chemicals. The end result reacted to a drop of water, burning fast, much like gunpowder.

"That's pretty cool, Clarence. What are you going to do with it?"

"Well, maybe I could put it around the drinking fountain?" He said to Ken. "A drop of water would hit it, and boy - would that really scare someone?!" Luckily this idea never materialized but Clarence didn't give up on his invention.

Saturday morning, Clarence, Ken, and Alice met up for a Debate Tournament at Central High School. The threesome slid across the seat of Mr. Bauer's Ford. With Alice seated between the boys and Ken driving, Clarence reached into his inside jacket pocket and pulled out a test-tube containing his water reactant explosive.

"Jesus, Clarence!" Ken exclaimed, "Aren't you worried about carrying that in your pocket like that? If you happen to sweat a little bit, that's liable to go off."

"Oh, no - hell no," he held up the test-tube, "see, I've got a tight rubber stopper in there."

Alice raised her right eyebrow and stared at Clarence.

Ken simply took a deep breath. "Ok," he said to Clarence.

Clarence returned the test-tube to his inside suit jacket pocket. A moment later, the car fills with smoke!

The passenger door flies open and a smoking Clarence whizzes out of the car! He hits the pavement, rolling in a cloud of smoke!

The car screeches to a halt. Horrified, Ken and Alice leap from the car and standby helplessly watching their friend thrash about.

Clarence rolls around some more, pounding on his chest in one of Omaha's busiest streets. Cars swerve. Horns honk. Traffic begins to back up. Meanwhile, Clarence is still smoking!

Once the chaos subsides, a heavy breathing Clarence looks up at his speechless debate partners.

"Jesus, Clarence! Are you ok?" Ken asked.

"Define OK."

Clarence was spared injury. His pride was not so lucky. The three teens return to the car.

Ken noticed a smoldering hole in Clarence's tweed jacket which had gone through to his shirt. His tie was burned off about two inches below the knot! Clarence looked a fright.

Ken had a pretty good idea of what had transpired, but he asked Clarence what happened anyway.

"Moisture got into my concoction and it exploded, blew out the stopper and turned the test tube into a rocket engine. A second later, the flame from my pocket rocket already burned through my jacket and cut my tie clean off." He held up what was left of his tie. Ken and Alice looked at each other and busted out laughing.

Not nearly as amused as his debate partners, Clarence sulked in embarrassment.

Ken composed himself long enough to look over at his friend. "Do you want to go home and change?"

"Naw, we don't' have time." Clarence played with the burned stub left hanging around his neck. "Maybe this ain't so bad." He finally joined in on the laughter.

The three debate students surprisingly made it on time to the National Debate Tournament.

"How are we going to get you straightened around, Clarence?" Ken asked his friend.

"Well, I suppose I'll just have to go like this."

When it was time for the threesome to take the stage, Ken and Alice studied their friend. Clarence made his way to the podium.

A curious audience watched as the young debate champion adjusted his scorched nub of a tie that hung from around his neck. Ken and Alice held their bated breath; they could only imagine how their friend would react considering the events that transpired earlier.

But as Clearance appeared before the sea of faces, wearing a dirty tweed jacket adorned with a burn hole through the shoulder and a matching burned neck tie, he confidently stepped up to the wooden podium.

"Ehhhh, ehhh, emm" Clarence cleared his throat and adjusted his tie, "You know, a funny thing happened on the way to the Debate Tournament . . ."

Invention of the '42 Motor Home

1954

Once he was out of high school, Ken realized two important things: first, he had an arsenal of extraordinary memories to look back on, and second, that his mother must have sensed kismet when she gently nudged her son in Alice's' direction when they met at a PTA meeting.

The two were inseparable throughout their junior and senior years in high school; Alice even turning down a full scholarship to Northwestern University to remain close to Ken. They were so madly in love that they couldn't wait to start their own family.

For several years after high school while they focused on their growing family, Ken worked several jobs to make ends meet. After graduating in June of 1952, he attended college during the days and worked evenings at Omaha Production Co. making hydraulic pumps. He also sold Fuller Brushes between his classes and tried to get his homework done on his thirty minute lunch breaks at the hydraulic company.

Ken struggled to keep up with all the commitments in his life. Soon the classes that used to be a breeze for him in high school became daunting and he decided that college would have to wait.

Somehow he managed to smooth-talk his way into financing a brand new car at the local dealership. Shortly thereafter, he lost his job with Omaha Production Co. Answering an ad in the paper, Ken rolled up in his brand new 1952

Nash Statesman hardtop for an interview to sell baby furniture.

The owner, Lee Anderson, was so impressed by Ken's new car that he hired Ken on the spot. The two wound up becoming lifelong friends and business partners in many ventures.

Once Ken addressed his financial needs, it was time to start having some fun. The young Bauer family had grown to the point where Ken wanted to provide bigger accommodations for their outdoor adventures. As the pioneer type, he hatched a plan to convert an old school bus into a camper. It could be argued that Kenneth Bauer invented the first RV unit of his time.

Ken and Alice enjoyed taking the kids camping and fishing. However, driving a family of five any distance from home proved to be a bit of a challenge. One of their favorite spots happened to be Lake McConaughy, located by Ogallala, 300 miles west of Omaha. Traditionally they camped there with the kids in a large tent.

During one outing they experienced a terrible rainstorm. All five of them huddled in their tent; miserable and wet, while Ken and Alice passed the time playing Monopoly in an effort to keep the kids from driving them crazy. They made the best effort to enjoy themselves; truth be told, they did not.

After they returned home, Ken wrung out and put away the weekend camping and fishing gear while he shared his story with his good friend, Lee.

"Oh, that was miserable," Ken said to Lee as he sorted through his tackle box, telling him about their weekend camp trip, "terrible for everyone."

"I'll bet." Lee unfolded a metal lawn chair to listen to Ken's story. He took a seat to watch the Sunday sunset from the Bauer driveway. "Kenny, what you need is a camper. Something you could drive the family around in. Something big enough that you could also load up all your gear, and maybe even pull a trailer behind so you can take your boat fishing."

"What are you thinking, Lee?" Ken was curious.

"Let's look in the paper and see if maybe you can find something you can make a camper out of." Lee offered. "Like maybe a van, or a truck or something like that."

As dusk sat in, Ken closed up his tackle box, folded the lawn chairs up and put them away in the garage. Lee was invited for dinner, and afterwards, Alice found the want ads for Ken. He and Lee sat at the kitchen table to look through the newspaper.

There it was! The answer to Ken's prayers was right there in black and white: a 1942 Chevy school bus. The guy wanted the outrageous price of $110. But Ken decided it was what the family needed. The next morning, Ken and Alice drove to meet the man and after bargaining him down to $100 Ken drove his school bus home.

Over the next several months Ken, Alice, and Lee worked on remodeling the bus. The first thing they did was strip the seats out of it. Ken found an old Servel gas refrigerator in the dump. He installed that and Alice found a 4-burner stove from a restaurant. They located some old metal cabinets at the dump. After installing their cabinets, Ken made a trip to the Military surplus store and bought some bunk beds; the old military style with flat wire springs connected to the edges and covered with 2 inch thick mattresses. The kids loved them because they were incredibly bouncy. Ken allowed as how this was going to be much better than sleeping outside in that tent.

Ken finally got the bus road-worthy. On a Saturday, the Bauer's drove the bus 300 miles out to Lake McConaughy to go fishing and camping for the weekend. The next morning they woke to pouring rain; a storm similar to the one they experienced in their last tent outing.

Ken, Alice and the kids sat in their bus playing board games, popping corn, and looking out the window at some soaked campers nearby in their tent.

"I think this is the way to go!" Ken said to Alice, proud of his accomplishment.

On the journey home, the engine overheated. Ken pulled over and used water from the fresh water tank he'd installed, to put into the overheated radiator. This got them all back home safely.

"Looks like a crack in the engine block." Lee told Ken the next morning as they peered down into the large cavity of the bus's engine compartment. "See that crack?" Lee pointed at the block. "Probably cost you around $100 to get you a new motor."

"A hundred bucks?! Hell, that's what we paid for the whole bus! Nah, a few hours with my dad's welder – and I'll get the job done."

Ken parked the bus in the front yard under the walnut tree. Next Saturday at the crack of dawn, Ken started working on the engine.

By noon the engine was hanging from the tree with Ken carefully welding the crack on the cast iron block. Several hours later the engine is back in the bus, and Ken is looking forward to fishing tomorrow. But first, he needed to test drive the bus.

By dinner the bus limped back from the test drive and exhaled a large puff of overheated vapors. The block cracked again; in the same place. Ken parked her back under the walnut tree, lifted the motor out again, and began a repeat surgery until late into the night.

Ken's father lived next door. The next afternoon he noticed the engine hanging from the tree for a second time that week and decided to investigate. Mr. Bauer approached the mechanic under the walnut tree and observed quietly for a few minutes before speaking up.

"Son," he interjected with some fatherly advice, "you know, back in the Depression when people did stupid things like this," he grinned at his boy, "we used to drill holes in the crack. Then we would thread the hole and screw in a brass screw and break the head off. After that, we'd drill another hole that overlapped that one," he demonstrated with his hands, "and thread it and so on. That way you'd have overlapping brass screws in the block, holding the crack together."

"That's a great idea, dad." Ken said. "Thanks, I'll give that a try."

It would have been an extraordinary plan; except that Ken had welded the block and hardened the metal. Trying to get those holes into his engine block was like drilling into the hubs of hell.

Ken spent the week selling baby furniture by day and drilling holes by night. But he got the job done after a lot of sweat, swearing, and broken drill bits.

By the end of the week, Ken was nearly done. At 2:00 a.m., with his engine still hanging from the walnut tree, his father decided to pay him another visit.

"Now what in the hell are you doing?" His father didn't appear to be in the advice dispensing mood this time around.

"I'm putting this engine back in here." Ken said to his father.

"Why at 2 o'clock in the morning?" It seemed to be a fairly legitimate question.

"Well, the reason is because we're going to lake McConaughy in the morning and I need to have this bus finished by 8 o'clock." Ken said to his sleepy eyed father. "I have to get it done, dad."

Mr. Bauer was quiet for a moment. Then with his tired voice he said to Ken: "Either you are the stupidest man I ever saw or the bravest." He looked up at the dangling engine and continued, "I wouldn't drive that goddamn thing across the street and here you are going to take it across the state." Mr. Bauer shook his head, tightened up his robe, and walked back to his house.

Ken finished on time for their adventure that morning. The Bauer clan drove to McConaughy, fished, camped and had a good time. Then the engine overheated on the way home. So they went through same process again by draining water from the tank to fill up the radiator. Ken was not surprised when he discovered that the block had broken in the same place, yet again. This time, when they got home, he would try a new angle and put some block seal down inside.

He purchased a case of block seal and poured all of it into the radiator. The grey chemical ran into the radiator and foamed out through the hole and Ken figured it would dry up and seal the block.

It slowed the leak in the block and plugged up the radiator. He back-flushed the radiator and hoped for the best.

He allowed as how if the block was leaking water – all he needed to do was have more water available than what was in the radiator. He converted a junk yard furnace heater into a thirty gallon tank to supplement the three gallon radiator.

So he mounted the tank onto the roof of the bus, ran a hose from the heater to the top of the radiator, drilled a hole in the radiator cap, forced a hose down into the radiator, and installed a valve next to the driver's window. This way he could ride down the street and every time the engine started to heat up, he would simply reach over, unscrew the valve a little bit, and water would go from the side arm heater down into the radiator.

Mission Accomplished!

White Dog Falls

1961

    Thanks to the enumerable efforts Ken invested in the motor home, the Bauer's were able to conquer several family outings. One of the most memorable trips was to White Dog Falls, Canada.

    Earlier that summer, Steve flew in from Los Angeles, CA to spend part of the summer with his aunt, uncle, and cousins. Between moving houses and transporting fireworks in a flammable fabric covered airplane, Steve had been introduced to the perils of Uncle Ken. He determined that a trip to Canada with Ken's homemade RV could only pale in comparison.

    The family's Canadian trip was soon underway. It seemed Ken's contraption was doing the trick as they drove through International Falls and into Canada. Soon they passed Kenora and the little Indian village that was the last stop before their destination: White Dog Falls Dam on the English River. Some of the best fishing Canada had to offer was near the dam.

    Traveling on the gravel road to White Dog, the bus suddenly swerved out of control and Ken had to stop. The left front wheel had fallen off and they thought to bring everything except a tire jack. With no jack on board, Ken and Steve improvised.

    They went out into the woods and cut down a tree with the right diameter that would be strong enough to lift the bus and long enough to gain the right leverage.

They placed the tree under the axle using a large flat rock for a fulcrum. Sure enough they were able to lift the bus! They quickly employed Alice to round up flat rocks that would fit under the axle as they lifted with their tree jack.

Once the wheel was off the ground Ken noticed the spindle that holds the wheel onto the bus had broken and there was no way it could be put back together. Ken needed a new front wheel spindle.

The odds of finding a spindle in Canada for a '42 Chevy school bus, in 1954, weren't going to be good. With the bus parked in the middle of the road, Steve stayed behind with Alice and the kids while she went inside to make lunch. Meanwhile, Ken began his journey on foot to Kenora (about sixty miles back) to find a spindle.

He hitched a ride into Kenora and searched in the only two junkyards in town; they had nothing like Ken's spindle. He started thumbing a ride toward International Falls and a man picked Ken up just outside of town.

"I'll bet you're hungry hitching down the road like this." The man said while Ken climbed in the front seat.

"Yes I am." Ken told his driver.

"Let's stop up the road a bit and get a sandwich." He suggested. Half way between Kenora and International Falls was a little restaurant with a gas station attached.

The two men entered the diner and took a seat at the counter next to a man having a cup of coffee. After ordering lunch, Ken noticed the name of the gas station stitched on the man's overalls.

"You own the station next door?" Ken asked the man in the greasy blue overalls.

"Yes, sir, I do."

"I see you have a bunch of old junk cars parked in the woods out in back of the station," Ken said, "are those yours, too?"

"Yes, they are."

"By any chance," Ken asked, "you wouldn't happen to have an axle for a '42 Chevy school bus, would you?"

The station owner laughed. "Naw, I wouldn't have anything like that."

Ken took a bite of his sandwich. *It was worth a try*, he thought.

"Now wait a minute," the man piped up, "I might have something."

Ken looked up from his plate with a spark of hope in his eyes. The man continued his thought.

"I got an old '42 truck that's been outta commission out there forever. It might have a spindle." He swiveled his stool to face Ken. "Maybe there's an outside chance it would fit a school bus."

The friendly man in coveralls stood to pay his bill and Ken was hot on his heels, thanking the man who gave him a lift on his way out the door.

He matched it up and sure enough – it fit! So he borrowed some tools, unbolted the part, and then paid the man a few bucks for the spindle.

Ken was amazed at his dumb luck finding this guy out in the middle of nowhere. He thanked the man profusely and started hitching back to the bus.

After he and Steve put the bus back together, the family preceded, event free, to White Dog Falls.

The next morning Alice strung up a clothes line to hang out the wet cloth diapers she had hand-washed in a large plastic tub and then rinsed out in a section of the fast flowing river.

Alice drove a pole into the ground and ran a clothes line to the front and rear of the bus, forming a triangle. It was soon full of clean diapers and the wet life jackets after taking the kids for a romp in the shallows.

Meanwhile, Ken was trying to figure out some way to have a private location for their 'portable' bathroom.

On the bus they had created a make-shift porta potty. It looked like a little camping chair, except instead of a canvas seat it had a toilet seat and they would hang a bag underneath to use it for a toilet. The problem was that having it on the bus didn't provide much privacy.

Ken soon came up with a great idea. First, he ran guy wires off of the pole. Then he found an old piece of canvas and wrapped it around the tri-pod in the middle of his wife's clothes line. This made a teepee, providing a private place for the porta potty.

Steve was the first one to try it out. Unfortunately for him, while he was visiting the outdoor bathroom, the wind came up. With all of the weight on it, Alice's clothes line came crashing to the ground, leaving Steve tangled in tarp, pole, porta-john, and rope. Ken stood nearby with an axe in his hand, laughing at the spectacle.

Poor Steve struggled there with his head and shoulders sticking out of the top of the fallen mess, trying to hold up the tarp debris, and his dignity, all at the same time.

Alice being the concerned aunt came running out of the bus to help her nephew – camera in hand! That photo became an instant classic in the Bauer photo album.

It seemed that once all the kinks were worked out from under the hood, the floodgates for fun were free to swing wide open! The Bauer's went on many more "Motor Home" camping and fishing excursions over the years to share in innumerable laughs and good times.

Learning to Ski

1958

    Ken landed a job with Celotex, a building material manufacturer. The Bauer's relocated to Duluth, Minnesota. Ken found a charming log cabin on top of a hill where they could walk right out their back door to a heavily wooded area and watch the deer come and eat from the apple trees in the back yard.

    Ken's sales territory with Celotex started at the Canadian border and stretched over 200 miles south, extending from the Eastern quarter of Wisconsin to western Minnesota.

    After spending several nights in motel rooms with nothing much to do, Ken allowed as how he should take up skiing. He fantasized about lit ski slopes that he could practice skiing during the evenings.

    Once he found a pair of skis advertised in the Sears catalog he decided on the perfect set. He ordered them, along with a pair of ski boots and poles, and all of his toys arrived at his home; assembly required. With anticipation, Ken assembled the ski bindings to the wooden planks and headed out to the snowy driveway to try them.

    The driveway sloped gently toward the street, making the perfect bunny slope. Ken stood at the top of the driveway with the ski tips pointed down, but he had to use his poles to pull himself down the hill.

    Obviously he needed a steeper hill. That hill existed on the main road, just off of the Bauer driveway.

    At the top of the hill Ken pointed his ski's downward, fully expecting the grade to pull him forward but it was like

Velcro – he didn't move an inch! Clearly he needed an even steeper hill.

Ken built a flying saucer slide the previous week on the back side of the property. The kids slid down it so many times that it was like a groomed slope. So he quickly headed for the saucer slide in back of the house.

Ken stood at the top of the steep saucer slide and pointed his skis downward. The second he leaned forward and pushed out over the edge, he knew this hill would work… too well.

He wobbled enough to force the ski's downhill, picking up speed so quickly it was as though he'd been shot from a cannon! OOPS! It is not a groomed slope. It is an icy luge!

Ken immediately turns the ski tips inward to slow down. Per instructions, he shifts his weight to the inside edges of the skis. The skis scrape hard against the ice as he continues to accelerate down the hill. The wind gets louder, eyes tear. The ski tips cross; still accelerating.

Now descending at blurring speed, the little shrub at the bottom of the hill is now a big bush right in front of him, still accelerating. With his tips crossed, Ken hits the bush, jams his ski tips inward, sails head first over the bush and tumbles ass over tea-kettle down the remainder of the hill in his best *Agony of Defeat* impersonation.

In the end Ken was laid out, looking like a snow man gone terribly wrong. His equipment formed a debris field on the slope above him.

With two twisted ankles, Ken crawled back home with skis and poles in tow, pissed that Sears sold him skis that stuck to snow. When he arrived at the front door he was too exhausted to knock.

Alice answered the *scratching* at the front door to find Ken with his skis lying behind him in a mangled pile.

She helped him into the warmth of the house and he told her the tale. The next afternoon he sent his skis, boots and poles back to Sears.

The following week Ken shared his skiing adventure with his friend Larry Hiuka, an avid cross country skier.

"Have you ever heard tale of someone who sells skis that stick to snow?!" Ken asked.

"Did you wax da skis? Larry asked in his Finnish accent.

"No."

"If you don't wax da skis, they don't slide, septin maybe on ice if you are stupid enough to try dat!"

Charlie Radford gets Married

1959

While Ken worked for Celotex selling building materials to lumber yards around Minnesota and Wisconsin, he met and befriended Charlie Radford.

Charlie was the son of the president of the Radford Company; the company Ken set up to serve as a distributor so he could drop ship orders of Celotex products being sold to the lumber yards in Minnesota. Ken and Charlie became good friends; they swapped stories, played pool at lunch time, and fished together as often as they could.

After dating Roberta for a while, Charlie fell in love and the two decided to get married. Ken was honored when his friend asked him to be his best man.

The two friends headed out in search of rental items for the upcoming wedding. After wandering around town, Charlie ran across a glass punch bowl.

"I suppose I'll need one of these to drink punch at the reception."

Ken's eyes sparkled as brightly as the crystal, remembering an artist on television carving a beautiful swan punch bowl from a block of ice. "No, you don't have to do that," he said to Charlie, "I can make you one of those."

"How the hell are you going to make a glass punch bowl?"

"Just trust me," Ken said, "I can do it."

Carving the swan looked so easy on TV, Ken did not even bother to practice before the wedding.

On the morning of the wedding Ken picked up the 100 lb block of ice and new carving tools. He delivered the ice to the church and set it up downstairs in the reception hall on a table.

Turning the ice around and around, he pictured a beautiful swan in his mind and began looking for it in the ice. He started to chip away at the ice thinking, *I'll just remove everything that is not a swan. How tough could it be*?

A rectangular head and neck soon took shape, then the body. He started shaping the head and neck and soon a little head was displayed on top of the neck.

Excited his swan was taking shape, Ken started to chisel details on the neck. CRACK. The neck and head plummeted to the floor and shattered!

"Oh my God, what do I do now? How in the world do I glue ice together?" Ken said under his breath. While the decapitated swan dripped on the drop cloth Ken wondered what he could do to fix the bird.

Ken had a revelation, *if I change the base of the neck into a head, I'll have a duck*. Panic set in as Ken realized he had more ice to carve than time to get it done.

He frantically chipped, chiseled and scraped the ice, determined to finish the duck before the wedding. He chipped and chiseled and chiseled and chipped; ice shavings flying in every which direction.

Ken formed the body, carved the tail, finished the little duck head, and hollowed the body to form a bowl.

Finally, he stepped back to admire his hard work. *Not too bad*, he thought nodding his head and smiling to himself. In the end, he turned a 100 lb block of ice into a 20 lb duck.

"What happened to the swan?" Asked one of the parishioners who had been setting up chairs in the other room.

"He turned into a duck." Ken answered. "What do you think?"

The parishioner stopped at the doorway with an armful of folding chairs to observe Ken's ice sculpting masterpiece. "A swuck." He offered.

Ken started to explain, but realized he was due at a wedding! He quickly covered his swuck and headed upstairs.

After the wedding everyone filed into the reception hall. He watched the guests dip punch out of his ice punch bowl to catch the expressions on their faces, looking for approval.

"How is it going, Ken?" Charlie asked, taking a break from all the congratulatory hand shaking. They were both looking at the swuck.

"What do you think, Charlie?"

"I, uh, – my punch is much colder." Charlie playfully raised his glass and winked at Ken.

"Well, look at that guy over there." Ken pointed to a man in line. He appeared to be studying his sculpture with great interest.

"Yes, he does seem to be curious." Charlie agreed. The man leaned to the right, then back over to the left, and then he hunched down to look at the ice sculpture.

He moved in closely, his face only inches from the punch bowl. He looked, looked some more, and then went around the other side of the table and looked from another angle.

"Now that guy is really interested in my carving – isn't he?" Ken announced proudly to Charlie. Let's go see what he has to say."

The groom and best man walked over to the punch table. "What do you think of that?" Ken asked the man.

"Well," the whisky breathed man said into Ken's face, "I was lookin' at it –" and he turns to observe the sculpture again… "It's a pig, ain't it?"

Charlie laughed in mid drink, spitting his punch all over the reception floor.

* * *

With Ken's feelings still bruised about the ice-pig, Charlie insisted that after the honeymoon, the two of them take a fishing trip. They decided to fish from the streams that poured down into Lake Superior.

"Why don't we just leave our shoes home and go in our chest waders?" Charlie reasoned.

"I don't see why not." Ken agreed, and the men loaded into the car to go fishing.

Up north toward the Canadian border, Ken and Charlie found their favorite wading spots. Unfortunately, when they arrived at their destination, the banks were muddy from the rains. At the conclusion of their fishing expedition, the two were unsuccessful in catching any fish, but they were successful in developing a remarkable thirst.

On the way back home they agreed to stop at Two Harbors, a little town north of Duluth. Inside of the American Legion hall, a thirsty guy could get a beer.

Pulling into the dirt lot, there happened to be more cars than usual. "Think we should go in there looking like this?" Charlie asked Ken. "There's a hell of a lot of people in there."

"Hell, we've been thrown out of better places than this!" Ken said. "Let's go in."

Inside of the old legion hall, pink and yellow balloons were tied to the backs of nearly every dining chair in the room. Kids dressed in their Sunday best; the boys in bowties and the little girls with ruffles and ribbons streaming from their hair. A half a dozen bridesmaids dressed in lemon yellow and pink satin gowns scurried about, giggling and fussing over the bride. Clearly they had wandered into a wedding reception.

They didn't mind. The two men found a table not far from the event, sat down, and ordered a beer. The band struck up and began playing polkas. A rainbow of colors flooded the glossy hardwood floor when the wedding party emerged to dance. Ken and Charlie smiled at each other.

"Ken you haven't got a hair on your ass if you don't go ask one of those pretty gals to dance."

"In these waders?"

"Well, you can take 'em off if ya want." Charlie teased.

"No, no…." Ken laughed back at his friend. He took a drink from his bottle and stood up.

The chest-wader clad fisherman strolled over to pick out one of the gals at the reception and asked her if she'd like to dance.

The girl Ken selected, giggled, and to his surprise actually said yes. A few steps in, he looked over at Charlie and motioned his head for him to go get one too.

The two grubby outdoorsmen spent the rest of the afternoon at the wedding party. Ken and Charlie were invited to drink their champagne, eat their cake, and dance the polka in chest waders with the bridesmaids at the Legion Hall.

Charlie successfully helped Ken forget all about his pig looking swuck.

Being back in Omaha and having such a great afternoon with Charlie reminded Ken how many incredible friends he'd acquired throughout his lifetime. None however, were nearly as treasured as those from his youth.

The Gatorbait Adventures

1947

During the Depression the Works Progress Administration (WPA) had projects all over the city. The WPA installed a storm drain system on Ken's street. Back then the curbs and gutters were constructed from sandstone blocks. The gutters moved the water to the low end of the street where there was a three foot deep, question mark shaped retention basin with a clay drain pipe at the deep end. The basin was about the size of a modern Jacuzzi.

The storm water basin fascinated Ken and his friends Donnie, Dan, and Gatorbait. So of course they spent several hours investigating and discussing what they could do with it. Upon further inspection, the boys discovered that if they plugged the pipe, the hole would fill up with water creating their very own pool.

So that's what they did. They plugged the hole one day after school and then waited for a long hard rain. Since it was October they didn't have to wait long, the hole filled up and they had their very own pool.

Even though they were excited about the prospects of this pool, they didn't really know what to do with it. So they claimed it like a conquistador would claim the fountain of youth. The water was too cold for swimming, so they soaked their feet in it. Then their feet got cold, so they built a fire to warm them back up.

This became the new hang-out spot where they spent their afternoons and evenings during the unusually warm fall. The boys would talk, scheme, joke and play into the evenings while moving their feet from water to fire and back.

One evening while Ken, Donnie, and Dan congregated at their pool, Gatorbait showed up with a 2-inch piece of iron pipe measuring about 6-feet long.

"Look what I found." He said. The plump teenager held the pipe over his head and fist pumped the rod into the air.

Donnie and Ken were sitting on crates with their pants rolled up; their bare feet soaking in the pool. Dan sat off to the side poking around at the fire pit to stoke it.

"Cool," Ken said, "whatcha gunna do with that?" he asked Gatorbait.

"I dunno, let's put it in the fire and get it hot on the end." He sat on the other side of the fire from Dan and dropped one end of his iron pipe down into the fire, burrowing into the hissing, orange embers.

The night air was still and quiet and the boys sat mesmerized by their firelight.

The gang silently observed. Sounds of their crackling fire and the creaking wood from under Gatorbait's behind accompanied them in the darkness. It came as no surprise to the boys when, sure enough, the iron pipe was red hot when Gatorbait finally pulled it from the flames to show everyone.

Proudly he held the pipe upright, pointing the glowing end toward the stars. "HEY, maybe this will warm up the pool!" Gatorbait announced. "Pull your feet out and let's see if this works!" The boys did as they were instructed, excited with possibility.

Gatorbait plunged the red hot end of his pipe down into the water and the steam erupted out the other end of the pipe like Ol' Faithful!

No one expected such a show. Of course this ignited Ken's imagination from a dim flicker to a full flame! "Wow! That was really something!" Ken exclaimed. "I wonder what would happen if we plugged the end of that pipe?"

Like watching a Fourth of July firework show, all of the boys' eyes lit up simultaneously.

"Yeah." Gatorbait said, nodding and looking around at the others.

"Here," Ken said, reaching out for the pipe. Holding the center of the pipe, which surprisingly never got hot, Ken slammed the cold end of the pipe into the mud, creating a solid plug about three inches thick .Then he hurried back over to the fire pit where everyone stood around in anticipation.

He stuck it into the coals to heat it up again. Once it was red-hot the foursome shuffled over to the Jacuzzi.

The boys watched the bright red end of the pipe disappear below the water and then . . .

Khuufluuuuuunnnk! The mud plug shot straight out the other end of the pipe; a steam powered mortar disappeared into the night sky.

"Cool!" The boys giggled and scurried around in excitement all chattering at once about how amazing that was.

"I wonder if we could hit something with that?" Donnie asked.

Embarrassed that he hadn't thought of that first, Ken looked around his neighborhood for a target. Ah, ha! Grumpy ol' Mr. Craig was always grouching at them over something.

"I'll bet we could hit his house." Ken said, pointing at the house across the street.

The boys figured if they were going to decorate someone's house with mud pies, it may as well be the mean guy.

They reloaded their mud-mortar and –

Khuufluuuuuunnnk! They shot it in the direction of Mr. Craig's house.

After some practice, they could finally hit his house. Once they managed a few direct hits in a row, out came old man Craig onto his porch.

"What in the hell are you doing out there?" he shouted into the darkness. "What are you shooting at my house?"

If not for the giggles coming from the darkness, they may have gotten away with their prank. But now grumpy ol' Craig was headed in their direction.

And just as quickly as their fun had started, it ended – Mr. Craig, without a word, swiped the steel pipe right out of Ken's hands.

What had started out as an evening filled with giggles and mischief, had turned to silence and stars. But it didn't matter. Halloween was only a few days away and in their neighborhood the 'tricks' always started early.

* * *

Duke Callier lived a few blocks away from Ken. At the edge of his cornfield, near his back yard, was an outhouse that the boys had tipped over the past few Halloweens. Ken and his friends knew several things about pulling this particular prank.

One, they could successfully knock over the outhouse. Two, they had never gotten into trouble so Mr. Callier must not know who had done it. And three, they had the best route through the neighboring cornfields figured out so they could keep under cover.

What the boys didn't know was how hard it was on an outhouse every time they knocked it over. Once it came crashing to the ground the nails came loose, all the hinges came off the doors, and the boards buckled; it basically had to be re-built. This resulted in the second thing the boys were not aware of: Duke was tired of rebuilding his outhouse and this year he was going to be ready for his little tricksters.

The next evening after Mr. Grumpy had taken their pipe, they all agreed to meet at the edge of Mr. Callier's cornfield for the outhouse ritual.

"This is so much fun." Donnie said, jumping up and down to keep warm from the chilly fall evening.

"How many times you think we can do this before we get caught?" Gatorbait asked. He was struggling to pull up his pants over his chubby tummy.

"Awe, Duke is cool." Dan offered. "Even if he caught us, I don't suppose he'd tell our folks. Do you, Kenny?"

"I don't reckon he would," Ken said as he stuffed his hands deeper in his pockets. "Alright, let's get going."

"Last one there is a rotten egg!" Gatorbait shouted and raced off into the tall corn stalks. He needed a head start so he could keep pulling up his pants along the way.

The other boys followed, weaving in and out of the dry, crinkling corn stalks – peeking over the tops as they made their way closer to the target. Along with the sounds of batted corn stalks, muffled giggling could be heard in the cold, night air. They were getting close! And then, out of nowhere, came a blood curdling scream!

It was Gatorbait . . . he had disappeared!

The yard lights suddenly flooded the cornfield and the area near the outhouse. Duke Collier came out of his house wearing his baggy overalls and a red flannel shirt. He could hardly stand up he was laughing so hard.

The boys were looking around trying to find Gatorbait.

"Git me OUTA here!" a voice was coming from far off. They all exchanged looks at one another. Then Donnie looked down.

"Look." he pointed at the ground near the outhouse, "Look at that."

They could hear Gatorbait still whining, "*Ooohhh*, git me outta here!" Duke had pushed the outhouse forward a few feet off the hole. As Gatorbait ran up in the darkness, excited to be the winner of the race, one hand holding up his pants, the other stretched out in front of him to be the first one to touch the outhouse, he fell right in –

KERPLUNK!

While the boys stood there speechless, waiting for Duke to catch his breath from laughter, they looked down at poor Gatorbait covered in disgust. Finally Duke composed himself enough to speak up.

"You boys," he caught his breath, "better help him outta there," he said, wiping the tears from his eyes. He walked back toward the house to get his garden hose.

Kenny and Donnie knelt down and reached for their stinky friend. Pulling him out of the hole and getting the Halloween outhouse sewage all over them as well, they stood quietly, waiting for Duke to hose them all down.

Knowing that the water was ice cold, Duke found extra pleasure in thoroughly rinsing off the three boys. *Best Holloween ever!* Duke thought. He then turned off the water and invited the soaked boys inside to get warm.

"You boys come on in here and have some hot cocoa," he instructed, still snickering. "The missus'll get you some towels to dry off with," he was winding the rest of his hose up, "and I'll find some dry shirts for ya to wear home."

All four boys, three froze to the bone, headed toward the steps leading to the backdoor of the little farmhouse.

"What were you boys thinking?" Duke asked.

Gatorbait answered and Duke started laughing all over again.

"I didn't want to be the rotten egg."

The Exploding Mailbox

1959

One arctic Saturday morning, back in Duluth, Minnesota, Ken somehow managed to turn a simple request from a postal service worker into an incredible explosion. A sleepy little mid-west neighborhood was about to fall victim to a street-debris hailstorm.

* * *

"Whatcha got there?" Don shouted from the property next door to Ken. The neighbor watched the vapors of warm air escaping from Ken's mouth while he read a note that had been left in his mailbox. The sun attempted to break through the grey Saturday morning sky as Ken shouted back to his friend.

"It's from the mail-lady." He answered, folding the handwritten note up and slipping it into the back pocket of his jeans.

"Well come over and have a beer." Don offered. Ken nodded in agreement and began to *crunch, crunch, crunch* his way across the frozen snow to Don's house to discuss his dilemma.

Warmly nestled inside Don's home, the men open two beer cans and settled down on separate couches to stare at the flames licking at the smoky glass of the woodstove.

"What's the mail lady got to say?" Don inquired.

"Well, she's not very happy with me." Ken said. "She allows as how it's bullshit that she has to get out of her truck and walk to my mailbox in order to put the mail in it." Ken reported and then swallowed some of his ice cold beer. "She says if I don't move it back where it belongs, she's not going to bring me my mail."

"Oh, yeah?" Don snickered.

"I can't say as I blame her. It's cold as hell out there."

Don nodded in agreement. "You ever find out who ran your mail box down?" he asked, standing up with an already empty beer can that he crushed between his hands.

"No" Ken shook his head and stretched a leg up onto the coffee table. Someone had run into his mailbox and knocked it down several weeks ago and because the ground was frozen solid, Ken couldn't dig a hole to put it back where it belonged. So he stuck it in the snow bank and that is where it had resided since the hit and run.

"Don," Ken asked his friend who was behind him in the kitchen, "how do you think I can get down through that frozen ground and get a hole dug?"

Don returned to the living room with two more beers. He had no suggestions.

"You got a bar that we could drive down in there with a sledge hammer?" Ken asked.

"Yeah, but that ain't going to be big enough for that mailbox post. I'll tell ya what we need to do," Don flopped down on the couch next to Ken, "I got about a half a case of real old dynamite out there in the shed. It's so old that it's sweatin'."

"Oh, yeah. That would work! You think we can use it without blowing our heads off?"

"Ah, hell – no problem." Don shrugged confidently. "It's just a little post hole."

So for the next few hours, and several beers later, the two discussed how they could make a hole with a bar, deep enough to get some dynamite down in it.

"Maybe ¼ of a stick would do, ya think?" Don offered at first.

"Oh, it's old, I'll bet we could easy use about 1/3 of a stick." Ken said.

"I don't see any reason we can't use a full stick," Don determined after all of the beer had been drunk. They stood up from the coffee table, now littered with empty beer cans and headed for the front door.

They had to determine how, exactly, they would create the explosion.

"The only thing I have is electric detonators," Don said slipping on his coat.

"Do you have a generator?" Ken asked, pulling his hat down over his ears. He imagined the generator would have a plunger that would spark the detonator.

"No, I don't - We could do it off a battery." Don said while he led the way to the shed.

Inside of the dimly lit shack, Don pulled out a stick of dynamite and demonstrated how the sweat on the side of the sticks was really nitroglycerin. He ran his finger over the stick and flipped the nitro to the ground.

Bang! Bang! Bang! Each drop gently exploded on the frozen floor of the shed. The grown men giggled like teenagers with a secret.

With a stick of dynamite in one hand and the detonator in the other Don kicked the door open flooding the little shed with the blinding grey light of the day.

Don mumbled something about going in through the side of the garage.

"It's unlocked." He informed Ken and they walk into the dark building. Ken switched on the light and he heard Don's voice behind him.

"Hey, grab that wheelbarrow over there, Ken." He pointed with his head. "Oh, and throw in that car battery there on the ground next to you."

Ken loaded the battery as instructed and then hunched over to place both hands on the wooden handles. Squinting, he focused on the blurry image of his friend across the room and navigated toward Don. He stopped short of running over Don's large goulashes and Don placed the dynamite and detonator into the old yellow wheelbarrow next to the car battery.

Next, they began looking for their bar and hammer. After locating and loading their tools they aimed for the open door and Don led the way.

Crunch, crunch, crunch – their rubber overshoes followed behind the single wheel carving a trail from Don's garage to Ken's mailbox.

Arriving on the scene they proceeded with their plan; taking a sledge hammer in hand, they traded off pounding a bar down into the frozen ground.

Next, Don pushed the detonator into a full stick of dynamite and dropped it into the hole. Ken reached for the car battery and tested it with a piece of wire to see if it would work. Nothing happened, not even a spark.

"I think your battery is dead."

"Yeah. That sounds about right." Don remembered now why it was sitting on the garage floor.

"Well what do we do now?" Ken asked as they both looked around.

"Let's go take one outta the car." Don suggested.

"Nahhh, that's too much trouble." Ken disagreed, standing up next to the hole, "Let's just drive the car over here."

"Well, okay." Don mumbled, following Ken toward the Bauer Chevy Wagon parked out by Ken's garage.

Don got in the vehicle and turned over the engine to let it warm up while Ken slipped into the house to locate a 20 foot extension cord and cut off the ends. They met back by the post hole construction site.

The hood of the car was opened to expose its insides, while an extension cord lay quietly over the white, frozen ground. Ken hooked up the cord to the detonator, looked over at Don, and then carefully touched it to the battery.

KAAAABOOOOOOM!

Within seconds of the hellish explosion that created a hole extending half way across the street, probably 20 feet in diameter, the air was filled with flying debris. Dirt, snow, and rock shot dozens of feet into the air, leaving no filler for the damn hole after it was over.

Ken and Don dove under the car as the debris came raining back down, hitting the car like a spring hail storm. The car squealed every time a frozen missile landed, forming another dent.

After the last of the rocks touched down; *thunk, thunk, thunkthunk* – the two masterminds emerged to survey the damage. The car looked like it had been run through a hammer mill.

Alice heard the commotion and appeared on the back porch. "Should I call the police or an ambulance?"

"Oh, for God's sake – NO!" Ken shouted. "We're ok. We're fixing the mailbox."

She shook her head in disgust at the two neighboring idiots out causing mischief in the dead of winter. Rubbing her cold arms, Alice turned and retreated back into the warmth of their house.

Silently the two men looked at the hole; then at each other.

"How are we gunna fill that big goddamn hole back in?" Ken asked Don. "I can't even tell where the street was!"

Don stepped to the spot where the hole started and paced out about three feet.

"Well it was right about . . . here . . ." he pointed, "and that's where the mailbox should go." Don said. "But maybe you could move it back a couple of inches to this spot." Don kicked at the loose dirty ground.

"Alright. Stand right there and hold this." Ken handed the white mailbox post to Don. "I'll go get some dirt to put around it." Ken hurried off to get a shovel and look around for dirt, which was now everywhere and mixed with snow.

He found patches here and there to scoop up and shovel into the hole and tamp down. Then he gathered more snowy dirt to put around the mail box and pack down. Then both of the men attempted to cover the cavern that used to be the street.

"We have to get this filled so nobody knows what we've done." Ken handed Don the shovel and went to find another one to fill their hole.

Over the next few weeks the two neighbors continued to shovel in dirt, snow, and rocks. They fought with the snow melt and had a heck of a time keeping that hole in the road filled.

"Don," Ken would frequently show up at his door with the same request, "we've got to go out and scrounge some more dirt."

Once winter had finally passed, Don used his front end loader and dump truck to provide their final solution. He got a truck load of dirt and filled the hole, packed the ground solid with the bucket and sealed it with crushed rock.

Although Ken never asked Don to use any of his 'old' dynamite again, he did share with Don on several occasions how his explosives career had begun way back in high school.

The Junior Mad Scientist

1951

During his junior year Ken enrolled in his first year of chemistry class. After completing the course the young student approached the instructor and asked to be put to work in his lab.

Mr. Dubler, the high school chemistry teacher, scheduled times to have his new assistant set up various experiments for several other chemistry classes and was so impressed with the eager young Ken he would ultimately create an additional curriculum to accommodate his assistants time in the lab.

The new courses would become known as Chemistry III and IV offered to seniors only. However, what the good teacher hadn't completely thought through was the fact that Ken now had full access to the chemical room.

This put the curious natured student in possession of such items as charcoal, potassium nitrate, and sulfur, just to name a few. So it came as no surprise that the first thing Ken went to work on was developing gunpowder.

Such a laborious chore didn't take him long. Unfortunately, his creation didn't excite him as he had anticipated. The gunpowder wouldn't burn fast enough. He considered his many attempts and efforts. It was as though it needed to be contained long enough to make it burn fast enough to blow something up. This required a container that allowed pressure to build until the explosion occurred.

Ok, this was fun, but not the vision in his head; that vision incorporated the Chinese and their ability to make flash firecrackers, rockets, and bombs! Nor, as he decided, was the gunpowder nearly exciting enough – especially given the chemical cornucopia spread out before him. Certainly there was more bang for his buck somewhere here in this room!

Bored with the mediocrity of his first explosive concentrate, he moved on. Consulting the Encyclopedia Britannica he familiarized himself with the formula for nitroglycerin. Kenneth began to dream of mega explosions not possible with mere gunpowder.

Filled with a curious determination, he made his way to school to further his research on these matters that baffled him. There on the shelves of the Tech library, he discovered "Black's Encyclopedia of Secret Formulas and Processes". The name alone was a thrilling discovery; he felt like a secret agent in training!

Unable to check the book out from the reference room, young Ken spent his free time in the library with this magical book. He dove into the information and emerged sometime later, armed with a new chronicle of knowledge. He now had even more ideas on what to do with his new friend nitroglycerin! He felt as if he could implode with anticipation!

Boil, boil, toil, and trouble, Ken began one of a series of concoctions back in the high school chemical room. Methodically, his process began with one part this, one part that, a drop of this, add in a dash more of that, and so-on, and so-forth.

On the first take, it wasn't quite the explosion he had hoped for. The brown contents he created in the beaker bubbled around the glass bottom, grew, morphed, and then shot up to the ceiling. *Hummm?* Scratching his head, Ken calculated, deduced, and re-calculated some more.

Finally he understood that an exothermic reaction had taken place that generated heat; therefore he would need to allow for a cooling process. Realizing how late it was getting, Take Two would have to be done at home.

From deep within the basement, while his entire family unknowingly relaxed above him, the mad little scientist filled a red Folgers coffee can with ice and salt and placed it on a table. Next, he added the nitric and sulfuric acid in a beaker and put that down inside of the can. He then poured the glycerin into the beaker where the ice would cool it, ultimately turning it to Nitroglycerin. He would need more chemicals if he was to continue his experiments at home.

Kenneth wandered around the basement thinking to himself. *Well, I can get away with borrowing a few items here and there*, he considered, *for an experiment or two, but that's about as far as I could push that . . . wait a minute!*

The name of the brand on the bottles from the chemistry lab appeared clear in his mind's eye – Merc Chemical. They would certainly have enough chemicals for what he needed, and they would be listed in the phone book.

The next day after school, Ken rushed home to contact Merc Chemical before his folks got home from work. He sat down at the kitchen table and flipped through the tissue paper pages of the phone book. Locating the phone number, Dr. Jekyll contacted someone there at the company.

"Hello. I'm with Bauer Photographic Laboratories. We have just started up a little company and we want to do business with you! I realize you probably can't set up a credit account, but if you could set up a cash account and tell me how much the chemicals I need will cost, then I will send my kid down there with the cash to get them from you. Yes, yes, thank you very much!"

Ha! Let the experiments begin!

Posing as 'the kid', young Mr. Hyde picked up a 9 lb bottle of sulfuric acid, a 7 lb bottle of nitric acid, and a gallon of USP glycerin! How the red flags failed to fly can only be attributed to the fact that it was 1952, but regardless – young Kenneth was - for all intents and purposes - in business! Now it was time to call in some pals and get to work.

Clarence DeYoung and Dick Lozier volunteered. These green, scientific architects began the lengthy process of developing the best possible explosive man would ever know.

The first item on the agenda was to make dynamite.

Dynamite is made from nitroglycerin absorbed into Keysolger. Of course they had no access to Keysolger, so they substituted sawdust. After absorbing the nitro with the sawdust, they had to devise a way to test their fledging dynamite.

"How should we test this, Ken?" Dick asked.

"Well, how 'bout we take a little bit of it here, and we put it on this anvil. Then we'll just hit it with a hammer." Ken figured that if it didn't explode, well, it didn't have enough nitro.

"Ok." Clarence agreed and so they began the testing!

Disappointed that their product was not exploding, Ken upped the stakes and proposed that they add more nitroglycerin and introduce a dash of potassium nitrate! This would certainly make their dynamite more sensitive.

BANG! The concoction was perfect.

The next challenge was creating a detonator.

So, it was back to the magic book of secrets.

Buried in the pages of "Black's Magic Book", Kenneth discovered a recipe for mercury fulminate. This was his answer to a detonator. Not only would this stuff explode without being contained, but all that was needed was a flame or a spark to set it off.

This time he set up shop in his parents garage where a new batch of trouble was about to take shape. It was here that he began developing his mercury fulminate.

The process appeared simple enough by taking metallic liquid mercury and dissolving it in nitric acid. This mixture would then be dumped into Ethyl alcohol, similar to the drinkable variety, except this alcohol was denatured.

Now, the first batch turned out the same as the nitro glycerin. Young Kenneth dumped his mixture into the alcohol and nothing happened. He stirred, and stirred, and . . . nothing . . . it just sat there. So he pondered the situation, wondering what he had done wrong, mentally flipping through his rolodex of ratios and process, until - *pwshhhhhhhhh*, he heard the slow hissing coming from the beaker.

Ken saw the contents of the beaker bubbling, bubbling, bubbling - and seconds later - *BANG!* The quiet contents he had just been stirring had become instantaneously restless.

The chemical mixture blew clear out of the beaker – spraying all over the walls, the floor, even the ceiling. The garage was covered in granular mercury fulminate – and although this stuff was harmless while it was wet, once it dried out, the slightest spark would ignite an explosion.

Seconds passed before his brain caught up to his bulging eyeballs. With a sigh, he registered the explosive situation he was standing in the middle of there in his father's garage. He frantically began scrubbing.

Once he was finished cleaning up, it was time to try it again. Only this time he incorporated Grandma's sauerkraut crock.

This luminous idea involved a coffee can over the top of the beaker inside of the crock. This contained the mixture as it shot up into the coffee can, so that it was diverted back into the bottom of the crock where it would turn into mercury fulminate.

A brownish-gray mud appeared in the bottom. Ken carefully transferred the mud into a beaker, washed the chemical impurities from it, and poured it out to dry.

Next, he needed a broomstick handle and some magazine pages to create the dynamite sticks.

Ken and Clarence interlaced one page over another until they achieved a ¼ inch thick cylinder that slid easily from the broom handle. With a screwdriver, they pinched one end closed, and then inserted the dynamite.

Now for the exceptionally skillful portion of the program: with a wooden dowel, and much like poking a sleeping bear, they would tamp the dynamite into the tubes!

Slurp, slurp, slurp - the sound of the nitro glycerin could be heard down inside the tubes while the boys intently pressed on with their dynamite production line. Somehow, both Ken and Clarence completed their project and miraculously made it out alive and with all digits in their proper places. This was fortunate, because they still needed to create the detonators for their dynamite sticks.

Much like the broomstick handle, smaller cylinders were fashioned by using a pencil and the mercury fulminate was placed inside, making the final product look much like a firecracker.

Ken decided to purchase fuses from the local hardware store. With the dynamite ready for production, a test would have to be made.

"Here. Let's use this metal paste bucket. This should shoot at least a hundred feet straight up into the air!" Ken handed the bucket to Clarence.

"Where did you get this?"

"Next door at Junior's place."

With only a ¼ of a stick of their dynamite to try out, Ken lit the fuse and hustled back to stand with Clarence.

KABOOM!

"Holy. . .shit . . .did you see that, Clarence?"

"Yeah."

The silver paste bucket shot up as they had anticipated, but shattered into small pieces in mid air. There was metal bucket shrapnel scattered everywhere.

By now curious neighbors were trickling out into the vicinity of the boom to investigate.

"What was that?" someone asked.

"I don't know what the hell it was," Junior said and turned to the boys on the other side of his fence, "but I saw it go over Bauer's house."

Getting into the House Moving Biz

1960

Back in Duluth, Minnesota, Ken became good friends with his neighbor, Don Nelson, who was in the excavating business. One day Don pointed out an ad in the paper for some Veterans housing buildings the government had for sale. Don explained that they were metal duplexes, formerly used for housing veterans after World War II. Now they were up for bid in a sealed bid sale.

"What do you think about bidding on some of these, Ken?"

Ken flipped through the pages. "There might be a lot of money to be made."

The following day the two neighbors drove into Duluth to look at the buildings. The structures looked to be about 20 feet wide and 50 feet long and in very poor condition. They were sided with corrugated metal on the outside and were severely damaged on the inside.

"With all these lakes around here, they might make great cabins." Don suggested.

"Or even hunting cabins in the woods." Ken added.

On the drive home they convinced themselves that this was going to be a real money maker!

Ken borrowed $2,500 from his father and they bid that exact amount for all 12 buildings. It was like placing it all on black at the roulette table and they won. They were awarded the bid and now the proud owners of 12 metal duplexes.

The new business partners allowed as how the best way to sell them was to offer a package deal; sell them as delivered to the buyer's lot.

The next process was to contact a local house mover.

"Four hundred per unit to move 'em," the gruff old man quoted over the telephone, "and that's within 5 miles of Duluth." Ken and Don agreed and told the man they would be in touch.

Next they placed an ad in the Duluth paper advertising the houses for $2,500 - each moved to the buyer's specified lot. And the phone began to ring!

After selling the first three they decided it was time to schedule moving. Don called the old man back but his expression worried Ken

"I'm sorry, what? Oh, I'm terribly sorry. Alright then. Thank you."

"What? Wrong number?"

"No. He died." Don reported hanging up the telephone.

"He what?

"Yeah. He died over the weekend." Don said. "Now what in the world are we going to do?" They had called every house mover in a fifty mile radius and found there were none they could afford.

"We're going to have to try to move 'em ourselves," Ken said, "How tough could it be?"

They placed an ad in the Minneapolis paper looking to hire a house moving foreman, then hired the first one that replied. Their new foreman explained to them the importance of the equipment. The problem was they had no equipment, nor the money to purchase any. So they decided to make it themselves.

Don located some old truck rear axles, complete with tires and wheels, and cut them in half with a cutting torch to remove the differential. Welding two axle shafts together made a saddle for the house moving timbers to rest on. The timbers had to be purchased, and luckily they had some money left from the down payments they'd collected on the three sold houses.

They ordered two 18" x 18" 60 foot structural select fir timbers that cost about $500 apiece. For a few hundred dollars more they purchased an old single axle truck tractor that still ran pretty well. Then they started looking around for a bunk that would attach the house moving timbers to the truck tractor.

They made a trip to the railroad salvage store to pick up two track jacks and other parts. Now they were ready to move their first house. Ken and Don successfully completed their first move, delivered it on time, and without insurmountable problems.

Somewhere between the challenge of being in a business that he knew nothing about, and the excitement of learning, Ken realized he had reinvented himself virtually overnight. For the next few months he and his partner sold and moved all of the Veterans housing duplexes and walked away with over $12,000 profit. This was more money than he had ever seen in his lifetime up to this point. That was the upside.

Ken had to make this business work because after his Celotex supervisor came to Duluth to visit him, and found him moving a house instead of selling building material, he was promptly fired.

This downside didn't phase Ken. Once they finished moving all of their duplexes he and Don began moving small residential homes. They quickly discovered they were not nearly as lucrative. All parties agreed they had to do something different.

The state of Nebraska was in the midst of clearing a right of way for the new interstate Highway 80, and as luck would have it, they were auctioning off all of the houses in that right-of-way.

Ken believed this situation would allow his old techniques of buying the house and selling it delivered onto the buyer's lot.

Ken and Don decided to divide up the equipment and part company. The Bauer's moved back to Omaha and thus began his house moving adventures!

Tri-Pacer Adventures

1960

Before the final move to Omaha, Ken found a Piper Tri-Pacer airplane for sale at the Duluth airport. He thought this was really a nice ship and made it his third airplane, and like his first, it was fabric covered. But it would be the first time he owned a plane with tricycle landing gears.

"These are much better than tail wheels," the salesman told Ken, "because you have a much better view of the runway on takeoff and landing."

Equipped with all modern conveniences, Ken had an electrical system complete with radios and an electric starter, and a constant speed prop. This allowed the pilot to adjust the pitch of the propeller to give more power during takeoff, gain more speed, and stabilize the fuel efficiency at high altitude.

"You can buy this beauty for only $4,500. I'll take $500 down and we'll set you up on affordable payments for the rest of it."

"Well, I certainly can't pass up such a deal!" And with that, Ken ended up with his Tri-Pacer airplane.

At Christmas time Ken wanted to return home to Omaha and spend the holidays with his parents. He got Alice to agree to fly in the new airplane.

Three days before Christmas the Bauer's loaded their little family, including the dog, into the car and drove to the airport. The packing turned into a fiasco that placed them at the airport around 9 o'clock at night. The temperature gauge read 20° below zero.

When Ken climbed into the airplane and hit the starter the engine would not turn over. The cold weather made the oil so thick that the starter simply didn't have enough power to start the engine. He had the airplane towed to the hangar where they put an insulated blanket over the cowl and inserted a hose from a portable oil fired heater.

In the meantime the rest of the family loaded all of their baggage and Christmas gifts into the baggage compartment behind the rear seat. Then they loaded the kids and dog; three kids side-by-side in the backseat with Irish setter on their lap while Alice occupied the copilot seat carrying brand-new baby David in her arms.

Ken realized that they were probably way overloaded, but reasoned that if the airplane wouldn't fly they could always go back home and drive. After they were fully fueled Ken taxied out on the runway, set the propeller pitch control to full fine, and pushed the throttle forward to full power. The airplane seemed to stay on the runway a long time, but eventually flew.

Once he was off the ground he realized how much of that 10,000 foot runway he used but decided not to mention that little detail to his wife.

They climbed to 10,000 feet, which seemed to take tremendous amount of time, and headed for Omaha.

The sky was clear, but very dark and moonrise had not yet occurred. Once the moon peeked out they could see a white glow from the ground shimmering with snow.

The next problem that developed was due to everybody's breath icing up the windows. The plane had a defroster system that blew warming air onto the Plexiglas, but this only cleared two spots about 4 inches in diameter, one on each side of the windshield. Alice scraped a spot in the side window to help navigate. They had only the shape and size of the towns below to verify their position.

Ken planned the trip around his fuel stops, planning to fuel up at the midway point of their trip in Fairmont, Minnesota. Before they reached the point of descent into Fairmont, Ken realized that the runway was only 3,500 feet long. He was afraid that if he refueled there he would be facing three problems.

The first being that the aircraft would be as heavy as it was during takeoff in Duluth. The second was that the runway was less than half as long as Duluth. And the third was the temperature at the airport this far south would certainly be higher. All of these factors together might lead to a crash at the end of the runway.

Ken looked over his fuel gauges that read slightly over a half a tank of fuel in each wing. Fairmont was about half way to Omaha so he figured that if he ran out of fuel, he'd have 10,000 feet in which to glide, so he could pick a field and safely land. As Ken got closer to Omaha, his fuel appeared to be going down much faster than it had on the first part of the trip.

About 25 miles outside of Omaha both tanks were reading empty. From experience Ken knew the tanks would have a certain amount of reserve but he didn't know how much. He decided to run the right tank empty, switch to the left one, and after a little bit, start looking for a flat field to glide down into.

Once the right tank ran out and he'd switched to the left, the lights of Omaha appeared in the distance. Ken radioed the Omaha Tower and asked them to turn the strobe lights on at the end of the runway and give him a straight-in approach. They complied.

Ken fully expected the engine to quit at any second but as the minutes crept by, the plane went the distance to the safety of the Omaha airport. The Bauer family arrived in Omaha shortly after 2 o'clock in the morning and Ken's folks picked them up at the airport to celebrate the holidays.

When Ken refueled the aircraft the next day, he discovered less than a gallon of fuel remained in the left tank!

* * *

In the fall of 1960, after Ken moved his house moving business to Omaha, he picked up a partner by the name of Lloyd Hedrick for a short time.

One winter evening, Lloyd and Ken found themselves in a small local bar, drinking a cold evening away sharing family stories.

"Ah, your folks sound alright, Ken." The more Lloyd drank, the more melancholy he became. "I ain't seen mine in quite a while."

"Where abouts do they live, Lloyd?"

"Not far. A little farm town in Iowa, just east of Omaha."

"Well, hell my friend. That ain't much more than an hours' flight in my plane."

"It's almost midnight, Ken."

"Well, we better get a move on if we're going to make it to the airport before we loose this buzz!"

Like most alcohol induced ideas, they seem so much better at the time they are conceived than once they are hatched. The two men arrived at the airport sometime before one o'clock in the morning and Ken flew to Lloyd's parents' farm.

Ken was most impressed that Lloyd was able to pick his parents' farm out of all of the others in the middle of the night.

"They have a pasture out there back of the barn. Think you could land there?"

"I think so."

Ken's void of confidence failed to impress Lloyd. "When I had a plane," he assured Ken, "I done it many a times."

In Ken's current condition he believed his drunken copilot. So he made a low pass over the pasture with his landing lights on and found it was completely snow-covered, but looked pretty flat.

He came over the fence on the second pass, chopped the throttle and landed on the ground safely. Ken taxied up to an area that was near the house and shut the plane off.

A very surprised elderly couple answered the door at 2 a.m. However they greeted their son and his friend, graciously inviting them to come in and sleep in the spare bedroom.

The next morning Lloyd's mother fixed them a nice country breakfast. Even through his hangover, Ken could see that Lloyd's father had something on his mind.

"How in the dickens did you guys land last night without killing yourself?"

"What do you mean?" Ken answered. "We just landed in the pasture and taxied up to the house."

"Yeah," the old man was still confused, "but how did you miss all of those bales of hay?" He pointed out through the large kitchen picture window facing the pasture. Ken swallowed hard as a mouthful of biscuits and gravy struggled down his throat.

The field was covered with huge bales of hay, scattered all about the pasture, and covered with snow. In their condition, neither of them had seen a single one.

After everyone finished breakfast, all three men walked out to the airplane. Lloyd's dad got his tractor and moved enough of the bales to give them a clear runway for takeoff.

From the air both Ken and Lloyd looked out the window at their tracks in the snow from the night before. Anybody would have thought they were dodging the bales of hay on purpose by the way the tracks weaved in, out, and around each one. Had Ken been sober, he decided, they would have crashed into one of those bales for sure.

"Wow, "Lloyd said to Ken looking at the tracks, "maybe we should reconsider our drinking career."

"I don't know," Ken hollered over the engine noise, "mine started pretty young."

"Oh, yeah?"

"Yup, down in the wine cellar when I was six years old." Ken and Lloyd shared drinking stories the rest of the way home.

The Wine Cellar

1940

Any six year old desperado worth a heck needs a good sidekick! Ken's happened to be his best friend, Donnie Wilson. Conveniently, these two rascals lived across the street from one another.

Ken grew up in a world where many of the neighborhood men raised gardens. Donnie's father, Andrew, raised and sold all kinds of things at a local market including big beautiful strawberries, gooseberries, and grapes. One afternoon a customer told him how to ferment his grapes and the conversation inspired Andrew to attempt his hand at wine making.

Several weeks later, once the wine making was complete, Mr. Bauer received a lazy Sunday invite to cross the street and imbibe with his friend Andrew over a gallon of homemade vino. With a jug of wine separating the two men at the kitchen table, their young boys played intently on the living room carpet with their lead Cowboy and Indian figures.

As Donnie's mother rocked quietly in the living room, busying herself with a needle point project, her husband entertained his guest in the kitchen. Andrew poured a small amount of the crimson-red liquid equally into to two short, pint sized Mason jars. He slid one over to his friend and the men proudly lifted their glasses.

"Euwwhh," Mr. Bauer wrinkled up his lips and nose and sat the glass back down on the table, "that's the sourest thing I've ever tasted." He slid his little Mason jar back to Andrew.

The boys quietly discussed their wagon-circle strategy to protect their people from the advancing Indians, while watching their fathers attend to their sour tonic.

"Here," Andrew rose from his chair to retrieve the sugar bowl from a lemon-yellow painted counter behind him and a teaspoon out of a drawer. He sat down again and with a steady hand, Andrew poured a stream of sugar into Joe's jar and then into his.

The men slouched comfortably at the table and stirred their drinks. Andrew in his denim bib-overhauls, a light flannel shirt and work boots, while Joe sat in a pair of khaki colored slacks, a loose cotton t-shirt and in his street shoes. They repeatedly filled their glasses with Andrew's pretty red juice, laughing and exchanging pleasant conversation for several hours.

A few days later, walking home from school, the kindergarteners recalled their silly fathers. A block from Donnie's house, they convinced each other they should go try some of that wine! The boys hurried their pace and rushed directly to the outside door leading to Andrew's basement.

Clamoring down the steps, the boys stopped at the collection of wine jugs Andrew had lined up on a clammy wooden shelf. Donnie kicked a milk crate upside down, and with his little five year old hands, he cradled the ceramic jug to pull it into his chest. Gently stepping off of the crate, Donnie placed the jug on the cold concrete floor between them and pulled the cork.

"Wait a minute," Ken reminded his friend, "we need to have sugar in here."

Donnie scurried back up the stairway, returning momentarily with the sugar bowl.

Donnie forgot the glasses and he was afraid to venture back into the kitchen so Ken devised another plan.

"Here," Kenny instructed his friend, holding the sugar bowl out to him, "take a mouthful of sugar. Then take a drink of wine."

Donnie's eyes widened with admiration; he loved Ken's idea! He grabbed the sugar bowl from Kenny and tipped it back until he felt the sweet, white crystals mound into a pile inside his mouth. As they slowly began to dissolve on his tongue, he reached out for the jug. Ken scooped it up with both hands and assisted the wine to Donnie's mouth.

Donnie drank the sweet concoction down and then with a hollow sounding thud, the ceramic jug met the hardness of the concrete floor. The boys exchanged a quick look at each other, and then giggled.

"That's not too bad." Donnie reported. "Your turn!"

Kenny started with the pretty porcelain bowl and poured sugar into his mouth. Shifting the little pile of sweetness around on his tongue, he reached for the wine jug. Donnie was prepared to help lift it to his friend's lips.

The two youngsters drank a considerable amount of wine that way. It didn't take long before the basement began to feel *different* and Ken wanted to go home. Both boys stared up at the stairs they had to maneuver.

One little foot after another, they made it to the top step and emerged into the daylight of the upstairs world and attempted to go their separate ways. The grass had become fuzzy, the trees weren't sitting still, and his front door felt miles ahead of him.

"Bye." Ken slurred.

"Bye." Donnie hiccupped.

Crossing Donnie's front yard, Ken vomited before continuing on his journey across the street to his own home.

With each step he felt the thick grapey-syrup writhing in his little tummy like a struggling animal coming up for air in quicksand. He vomited two more times before reaching his front door.

After winning a fight with his own screen door, little Kenny stumbled into the house where he was met by his robust, German Grandmother. Her blurry frame emerged from the kitchen and Ken's head swiveled above his shoulders in order to look up at her.

"AhhhhKkkk," an angry growl from the back of Grandmas throat was loud in Ken's ears. She wiped her flour covered hands on her apron, "Kin-ny, wat you do now?

"I . . . don't . . . know . . . Grandma. Something I ate." he managed to tell her, his voice sounding unfamiliar in his own ears.

The little boy weeble-wobbled down the hallway and with a victorious sigh, flopped down onto his parents' bed. This triumph earned him zero sympathy from the old woman.

Not long after he laid a throbbing head on the cool feather pillow, he heard the sound of his dad's voice.

"Where's Kenny?" Dad asked Grandma.

"AhhhhhKkkk," the disgust was clear in Grandma's snarling German voice, "he's in on dah bed . . . drunk!"

Part Three

House Moving Adventures

Introducing John Jerks

Ken remembers the following John Jerks events as they took place in the sixties; a time when our culture was not terribly sensitive toward racial prejudices or stereotyping. Therefore it is important to point out that during the writing of the stories involving John, there were never intentions of racial slurs.

The stories are told as Ken remembers them; affectionately and humorously. He tells the *Missa Kinny* stories in a way that captures John's thick accent, keeping the integrity of the conversations and the experiences intact. The dialog depicting John is not to demean, but rather to honor the memory of a very important man. This gentle giant was not only a valued employee, but he turned out to be a loyal and trusted friend until his untimely death to cancer in 2009.

Ken could easily devote an entire book to *Missa Kinny* stories. Instead, he chose several of his favorite memories to share while introducing the reader to an individual who is still near and dear to his heart.

* * *

1960

With the Bauer family officially situated back in Omaha, Ken's house moving business was really showing promise. This is how Ken and John first met. Ken needed help moving one of his houses and went in search of manual labor . . . he found John.

Hiring manual labor was quite a different process in those days. A man could be hired from the State Day Labor Office, affectionately referred to in the industry as the 'slave market'. This simply meant that a business owner could go down to the office, explain to a group of laborers what kind of work was available, and hire someone for a project or for the day. When Ken explained what was involved in moving a house, John was the first to step forward.

"I believe I could do dat," said the large, clean shaven black man, "my name is John."

"Alright John." Ken extended his hand and the 5'9" barrel chested man took Ken's hand in his. It appeared he had not an ounce of fat anywhere on his body and his arms were so long they nearly hung to his knees. As he shook Ken's hand, Ken realized that one of the big man's biceps would equal his entire thigh.

"I'm sure you will do just fine, John."

No one would have believed the sheer strength of John Jerks until he made a believer of Ken that afternoon. The two men rode back to the job site while Ken explained to John what they were doing.

The first thing Ken did was to take John down into the basement of the house they were about to move. At both ends of the basement he pointed out the large holes in each of the walls where they would be fitting the beams through.

"We knock holes through these walls . . . see here?" He pointed out to John. "Then we take that winch truck up there," Ken pointed and John looked through a window where the truck was parked up topside in front of the house.

"…and we take a carrying stick and put it in the back of the house on each side with the winch truck. Then we move the winch truck back to the front and I'll drop the winch line through the hole and you guys put it around those 12x12 carrying sticks." Ken paused for a moment and then continued the basement tour, walking John along through the process, pointing out each step.

"See these beams? They go in there and once they have tipped over the center point, we'll drag them along the floor with the winch until they almost touch the front basement wall." John was nodding and walking along with Ken as he watched the demonstration.

"Then you boys will build a crib underneath the beam and jack the thing up." Ken stopped to look at John who was listening intently. "When I see it come up through the hole I'll pull it through so it can stick out 2 or 3 feet.

"You got all that, John?"

John nodded his head.

"Ok then, you guys go ahead and build a crib and jack this up and I –"

"Uh, Missa Kinny?" John gently interrupted.

"Yeah, John." Ken figured he didn't absorb that entire process the first time around.

"Missa Kinny," he was still staring at the beam, "hows come you done jus let me pick it up an stuff it through da hole?"

Ken's two other employee's exchanged a look, smirked, and looked down at the ground.

"Because the goddamn thing weighs about a thousand pounds, John!" Of course it wasn't exactly that much, but it was in the ball park of at least six or seven hundred pounds. John continued to size up the beam so Ken figured he'd have a little fun with this guy.

"I tell ya what, John. Why don't you just do that? I'll get the truck over there and when I see it come up through the hole I'll pull it through. You just go ahead and stuff it up there." Ken says, walking away laughing to himself.

"OK, Missa Kinny."

Ken humors John and gets up in the truck, chuckling and laughing. *Boy, am I gunna teach this new guy a lesson*, Ken thinks to himself.

Only a few minutes pass before Ken's smile is wiped from his face. He sees the beam coming up through the hole! He couldn't believe it! He quickly winched the beam through the hole, and then sets the beam down to get out of the truck and run back down into the basement. The other two guys were standing there with their mouths open.

"Ok, how'd you guys get this lifted up there?" Ken asked.

"No, honest to God, Kenny," one of them spoke up, "John got his back under there and lifted it by himself!"

That is how the rest of the afternoon played out: John pushing the beams through the hole by himself and Ken dragging the beams into place. None of them had ever seen anything like it before. It didn't take long until it was time to move the house a few miles up the road.

This particular house had a brick front porch, so once the house was lifted and ready to be moved, Ken had John follow him down the street in the event a brick might fall off. On the last stretch of the journey, there was a hill they had to climb. The owner of the house had been watching the entire process and wanted to show his appreciation for what a fine job he thought they had done.

After the house was set into place, the man walked up to John to compliment him on the move. "I've never seen that done before." He said to John, "how do you keep from losing any of those bricks off the house?"

John wanted to make a good impression, so he explained to the man, "That's why Missa Kinny has me a walkin behind da house." He tells him. "They done sometimes falls off, but I picks 'em up – we never looses a single one."

The man smiled and nodded at John, uncertain how to properly respond to such an unusual explanation.

This was the first of many house moving adventures for John and Missa Kinny. The day John came to work for the North American House Moving Co. not only changed Ken's life, but also his repertoire of stories for years to come.

Winch Truck on yo Sofa?

1961

The angry phone call came in sometime around 10 p.m. By now, it was safe for Ken to assume that a phone call this late could only mean that John had a little trouble on the job.

* * *

Thursday morning started out so pleasant. Alone in his office, Ken enjoyed the silence of the new day until the inevitable first-knock interrupted his tranquility.

"Come in," he said through a sigh under his breath.

A large dark figure filled the entrance when the door opened. Big John entered through the door way. He made his way across the room and stood at his boss's desk. "Missa Kinny?" The big man said.

"Yeah John?" Ken didn't bother to look up from his newspaper.

"Missa Kinny, Al is a needun to move outa his apartment this weekend."

"Mmmhhm." Ken replied; still no movement from behind the desk.

John continued, "Well, is, uh, dare any way you would let us use dat winch trucka yours?"

"Yeah, John, that's not a problem." Ken flipped the newspaper to the next page. Satisfied, John quietly ducked back out of Ken's office. It was later that evening when Ken received a phone call about the borrowed truck.

"Hello?" Ken answered his telephone, wondering who on Earth would be calling so late. There was a shrill voice on the other end of the line.

"You da one dat got dis, uh, North American House Movin?" the angry woman's voice asked through the telephone.

"Yes" Ken answered, terribly concerned where this was headed.

"Yo damn truck is here in my livin' room!" She continued. The pitch of her voice had a thousand little pinchers that raced down into Ken's ears, burrowing into his eardrums.

"The truck is in the living room?" he asked her incredulously.

"Yeah," the squeaky angry woman ranted on, "that big ol long thing is sticking out there, and it got that long thinga hangin down right over my goddamn die-van."

Ken figured the best way to deal with this was to go see for himself what had happened. He asked the angry woman for her address and drove to her home.

Sure enough, just as she had told him - his winch truck was, in fact, backed through the front of her house. The A-frame boom on the back had gone right through her front window. It was the snatch block she tried to describe that was, indeed, hanging directly over her couch.

Ken looked around the house, and asked the woman, "Where are the guys?" His question settled with her like gasoline on a fire.

Squeeky shook her painted fingernails in the air and shouted, "Dare wadn't no guys, jus dat goddamn truck! It mussa run down dat hill and run right in my house!"

Ken needed to find the guys and figure out what had happened here. He left her standing there in her living room, hands on hips, a pink robe and slippers, mad as hell, watching as he headed up the hill.

Certainly John and Al must be up on the hill somewhere. Arriving at the top, Ken spotted a pub and placed odds that inside he would find John and Al higher than Halley's Comet. Ken walked in and sure enough, he spotted the two bellied up to the bar.

"Jesus Christ, John!" he hollered, standing right behind them. "Where's the winch truck?"

John jumped off his bar stool, nearly knocking it over. He pointed at the front door, "Right out here, Missa Kinny."

"You remember the emergency brake wasn't that good?" he reminded John. "Did you remember to put a block behind the tire?"

"I sho did, Missa Kinny, you betcha, that's gona be there, there aint nuthn wrong with dat."

"Come out here for a minute." Ken motioned at the two men. The inebriants trailed behind him, out through the front door of the bar and toward the street. The two surveyed the curb where they had left the vehicle several hours before.

No truck.

Ken shook his head at the two standing there looking up and down the street for the missing truck. He surmised that his winch truck had rolled down the hill backwards from the bar, picked up speed, slowly turned, and then went in right through that poor woman's living room wall - while John and Al sat at the bar sucking down a few suds.

Although Ken was incredibly mad at these two, he couldn't help but smile at the child-like expressions on their grown faces – as if they were trying to put the pieces together; wondering, now how did that happen?

"Come on you two." Ken said to the foggy-headed pair.

The threesome walked back down the hill. Squeeky, standing in her front yard in her pink hair curlers and bathrobe, was coming into view with each step. No doubt, still mad as an ol' wet hen. *This woman could sober the drunk off of any man,* Ken thought to himself. Maybe that won't be such a bad thing.

Arriving in the front yard, Ken faced the woman - with John and Al at a preferred safe distance behind him. Ken barely opened his mouth to speak to her, when she decided to let the winch truck drivers have a piece of her mind.

"You da ones did all dis?" Squeeky craned her neck around Ken to yell at John and Al who looked at the ground like a couple of six year old boys that just got caught smoking out behind the barn. "You put dat godamned truck through my window? I sho oughta kick yo ass!"

Ken feared the situation was about to get even more ugly. "Alright, let's figure this out," he said to the woman. He then turned to John and Al, "Say, you boys know how to hang two-by-fours so you can fix this woman's walls?"

John raised his eyes, but not his head, "Well, now, no, we uh, we don't know how to do dat, Missa Kinney." Al shook his head from side to side in agreement with his friend.

Squeeky's head was picking up circular speed. Her lips tightened and her nostrils flared in mounting aggravation. Ken realized that he better come up with something quick. "Well, how about this window," he asked pointing to where the winch truck had backed clear through, "can you take that window down and have it fixed?"

"Oh, now we might be able to do dat, if we can find someone to, uh, to put da glass in it." John answered.

Squeeky threw her painted fingernails into the air in total disgust. "I can't belive dis mess, an all you gots is deez two here dat done ran dis truck up in my house? And now yous spect these same fools to start a buildn my house back? Is you crazy? Why you cant spect nothin' from …." She trailed off and Ken realized this was going nowhere fast. While her voice carried off into the midnight air, he considered that she might have a point.

Since they were blocks from Al's apartment, Ken thought it would be best to get the truck and the boys off the scene before the police decided to show up. His only saving grace to this point was that she hadn't called them yet.

"Why don't you boys go on and get the truck pulled outta here, and I'll take care of this mess."

"Oh, okay Missa Kinney. I think dat might be a good idea." John agreed.

As the boys drove the winch truck out from the front of Squeeky's house, glass broke, wood splintered, and a pair of her sheer white drapes ripped from the rod and flailed proudly from behind the boom of the truck as it drove away.

"Oh my gawd, dem drapes was my mamas, you done messed up my whole house wid dat goddamn truck!"

Ken wanted to kill John and Al.

Out of ideas and wanting a few beers himself, he turned to Squeeky and said, "You know, maybe it might be best if I hire a qualified contractor to come take care of this for you."

* * *

Years later, Ken's son Marty asked John about this event. While working on one of his dad's paving jobs, Marty shared a room with John in a local motel. Marty took the opportunity to ask him about one of his favorite "Missa Kinny" stories that his dad loved to tell.

"John," Marty asked from the queen size bed closest to the window, "was that winch truck boom really sticking clean through that lady's living room?"

John lifted both arms and locked his hands behind his head and stared at the ceiling. "Nawh. Yo ol' man is saggeratin' 'bout dat. As I recall, it was in more closer to da kitchen."

Canadian Washboard Fishing Trip

1961

When the Bauer family relocated back to Omaha from Minnesota the only thing they left behind was the old '42 Chevy school bus. Ken made arrangements with some friends to park it in their yard and pick it up the following spring. With the annual Memorial Day Canadian fishing trip right around the corner and foremost on Ken's mind, it made planning easier, because the bus was already two thirds of the way to Canada.

Since Ken purchased his fabric covered Piper Tri Pacer airplane, it made the fishing adventures even more spectacular. For many years he tried to convince his dad to go fishing with him; Joe claimed he didn't like to hurt the fish. But Ken persisted, convincing his father to come along on their fishing trip and take some vacation time together.

The television news station forecasted intermittent storms in the Omaha area; fortunately Canada looked like nothing but clear skies. Ken's childhood pal Donnie Wilson, joined Ken and his father, along with another Nebraska friend, Jerry Greeno. At the airport all four men boarded Ken's aircraft. Jerry was not a huge fan of flying nor was he a huge fan of Ken's new airplane.

"I can't believe I'm flying in lightning with you in a Goddamed paper airplane." Jerry grumbled. The four men took off in the four-seater and flew the 500 miles into Duluth. Ken made arrangements to have his friends meet them at the airport and bring the bus so the foursome could spend the evening preparing for their trip.

The next morning Jerry and Donnie took off with the bus, while Ken and his Dad flew into Kenora where Ken arranged to meet them. The Bauer's waited at the airport for nearly four hours.

"They should have been here long ago." Ken said to his father after having a bite to eat. "They gotta be broken down somewhere." Ken allowed as how they should fly south in the airplane to see if they could spot them from the air.

Sure enough, there was the bus parked alongside the road about 60 miles south of the airport. Ken noticed Donnie and Jerry waving as he flew by.

"Looks like they're in trouble." Joe shouted to Ken.

"We'll have to land and go help 'em out."

"Land where? There isn't an airport around here, is there?"

Ken looked at the charts and sure enough there wasn't any. "Well, maybe we can find a road."

"Oh, hell Kenny, you're not going to go through that again, are you?!"

Instead of a road, Ken spotted someone in the distance on a grader. The operator had graded a strip out in the middle of the forest - it was like the finger of God - pointing and telling Ken: This is where you can land!

What Ken didn't know was the grader operator had stirred up the ground in that area, leaving loose sand about a foot deep.

Ken came in really low over the top of the grader and noticed him waving his hands. He thinks he's waving him in and he grazes over the top of the trees, chopped the throttle and dropped the airplane in the graded patch. They stop almost instantly.

"Oh, shit, that might be a problem getting this back out of here." Ken said and then hopped out of the plane to explain his situation to the aggravated grader operator.

"You goddamed idiot, I was trying to wave you off."

"Oh, I'm sorry – I thought you were trying to wave me in."

Ken and his dad hitched a ride back to the bus. Joe being the mechanical whiz, assessed that the problem was with the coil wire. He unscrewed the terminals, ran the wires back into place and everything was back on schedule. Everyone boarded the bus and drove back to the airplane.

"I need you guys to stop here because I think I'm going to need a push." Ken announced, telling them his loose sand dilemma.

"Dad, I probably won't be able to get the plane going fast enough to get it off the ground with both of us in there, so it's probably best that I go by myself."

Donnie and Jerry took a wing each and pushed forward while Ken gave the plane full throttle. It barely moved in the sand. They ran along side of the wings, pushing until the craft picked up enough speed to take off on its own, and then they finally let go. Ken took to the air.

His speed was slow and the airplane was barely flying as he came up on string of high trees at the end of the runway. *This is going to be scary.* The only thing he could think to do was to nose down and fly as level as he could in order to pick up enough speed to clear the trees. The hope was to yank it up over the trees at the very last second.

Joe stood on the ground, scared breathless, watching his son. It looked as though Ken was about to fly straight into the trees at high speed. Instead, at the last minute he zipped up over them and headed back to Kenora.

With everyone meeting up, the fishing trip began just north of Kenora on the Jones road. This road lead out to a couple of lakes Ken researched earlier on the map.

"How'd you come by these lakes, Kenny?" Jerry inquired.

Naturally, by the color of the map. Ken could tell which lakes were going to be deep and have lots of good fishing!

"Are you shitting me?" Donnie chimed in.

"Oh yeah," Ken reached for the maps in the glove box, "look here. They're great spots."

It turned out that the Jones road was a true washboard dirt road. The original road was built up over a swamp where they cut down trees to lay crossways over the mud, and then graded dirt over the top of the logs.

Several miles down the road the bus slowed its approach at a toll gate owned by a logging company. A guy in the booth wanted them to pay a toll to continue down the road. Donnie prepared to jump out of the bus and go pay the man.

"Joe," Donnie turned around to Mr. Bauer who was sitting on the couch, "I'm not going to pay for everybody and their gunna charge us per person. So why don't you go back there and hide." Ken's dad complied and shuffled off to the back of the bus.

Donnie paid the toll, visited with the local a while and walked up to the driver's side window. "Hey, can I have a ride with you?" Donnie joked with Ken.

"Yeah, come on in." Ken started the bus and the fishermen continued down the bumpy dirt road.

Joe had climbed into the one of the steel spring bunks built over the top of the wheels. So every time the bus would hit a bump it bounced his rear end up into the air, and then slammed it down onto the wheel well.

Bam! Bam! Bam! The tires managed to find every hole in the road. They carried on for several miles filling the bus with dust and conversation until Donnie realized Joe hadn't reappeared.

"Kenny I can't believe your dad's sleeping through this shit. Maybe we had better check on him back there?"

Donnie walked to the back of the bus and found Ken's dad . . . clutching the upper bunk springs. With bent fingers hooked through steel mesh above him, he looked like a cat clinging to a roof! He looked over at Donnie with a wild-eyed expression.

"Is he still in here?"

Donnie tried so hard not to laugh. "Who?"

"The gate-guy," Joe says, "that got in the bus."

"That wasn't the gate guy- that was me!"

Joe unwound himself and crawled out of the bunk. He could hardly move. Those few miles nearly beat the living shit out of him. He returned to the front of the bus and Donnie recapped so everyone could have a good laugh; including Joe.

The foursome made it to the lake in plenty of time to get some fishing done. With the sun at their backs, Ken got the map out to show his Dad where they were headed.

"Now, the thing you gotta remember here Dad, is we're going to have to do some maneuvering. There just isn't any way to get there, except to portage our boat over this little short portage here," Ken pointed on the map, "which leads into the second Lake."

"Why would you do that?" Joe asked.

"Because that's where the good fishing is." Ken answered.

"How do you know?"

"I just know, Dad." His aggravation mounted. He could hear Donnie and Jerry laughing into their tackle boxes.

After gathering all their tackle and un-strapping the boat from the roof, they attached the heavy motor and launched the boat. The men crossed the lake and now had to portage everything over a ridge and into the second lake.

Strangely, there was no trail leading to the portage. *Surely they were not the only people to portage into this lake,* Ken thought, keeping this observation to himself. Moreover, they were looking at climbing an embankment leading straight up a hill face.

"You can't be serious." Joe said. "We can't carry this boat up this mountain."

"Oh, it won't be that bad. We'll just get one guy on the front two in the back…you just take the tackle box."

After taking the heavy motor off, the three men carried the boat over to the embankment. They pushed and shoved and finally got it up over the mountain and down the other side. They made a second trip to fetch the motor and a third to carry everything else.

Once on the other side Ken said, "Now we're going to see some fishn'." They started up the motor, ventured out a bit, baited their hooks, cast their lines into the clear water and pretty soon they were trolling parallel to the hill they had just been climbing. As they cleared the tip of land, Ken's father pointed across the lake.

"Hey, what's that over there –"

"Where?" Jerry looked up from his line.

"Isn't that the bus?!" Joe said.

"Looks like the bus, but it can't be - we're in the next lake over." Ken said.

They had gone through all that trouble to portage all their stuff over a point and back into the same damn lake. Donnie looked at Jerry, the two of them looked at Ken.

"Only *my* son would do this." Joe said.

Although Ken knew his father was teasing about the enumerable cracks his son had managed to get his ass caught in over the years, Ken also knew how proud he'd made his father. He watched the sun dance off of the lake to reveal Joe's aging skin; Ken sat quietly, reflecting back to the exact moment when his relationship changed with his father.

Turning Point in the Rotary Club

1948

Becoming a model student at thirteen wasn't always high on Ken's priority list. Rather than the acceptable studious behavior, he preferred such activities as harassing the girls sitting in front of him, or telling stories or jokes to get everyone laughing. So it turned out as quite a surprise to him, one afternoon at school, when his name was announced to receive an award as one of two students nominated to the Rotary Club Honor Roll.

Of course, he thought this was a huge mistake and at any minute someone would figure it out and correct the error; but that didn't happen. So he allowed as how he would simply indulge the faculty.

Ken went around that afternoon telling his friends what had happened; laughing and joking about the mishap.

"What?" Donnie laughed, "You?"

"I know," Ken agreed, "what were they thinking? It's got to be a mistake. Wait until I tell my folks; they'll get a kick out of this."

But they didn't think it was funny. Not only did young Kenneth get an unexpected reaction from his parents, he ended up with a surprise of his own.

* * *

Ken's mother was employed with Goldstein Chapman's as a buyer for infant and teen clothing and Ken's father would regularly pick his wife up from work. After the gasoline rationing stopped in 1945, many people began relying on public transportation. Often, Mrs. Bauer would make plans for her husband drop a few of her girlfriends off on their way home; an arrangement we know today as 'carpooling'.

Something else that Mrs. Bauer orchestrated was a way for her son to earn some extra pocket money. Once in a while, Ken would work for his mother making boxes. He could spend a few hours after school putting boxes together earning him a quarter.

Ken liked working after school with his mom, as much as he enjoyed riding with his dad to pick up his mother and her friends. The day he received his Rotary Club nomination, Ken decided to ride with his father to pick up his mother; that would be a good time to tell his parents of the funny news.

With Kenny in the back seat, Mr. and Mrs. Bauer in the front seat, they all rode home together from the department store while Ken delivered the news.

"Mom, Dad," he leaned over the long blue vinyl front seat of the '48 Buick, "you won't believe what happened to me at school today." He began.

"What's that?" His mother asked him while his father produced a quiet grin on his face to let him know he was listening. Ken continued.

"You know how they pick two students each year for the Rotary Club Honor Roll?"

"Yes." His mother acknowledged her son while staring out the passenger window, her hands carefully folded in her lap.

"Well, they picked me." He let the words hang there in the car, fully expecting them to start laughing. "Can you believe that?" He asked. But instead of the laughter he expected, the look on his father's face was serious.

"I think that is just wonderful news, Kenny." His mother said, turning to look over her left shoulder with a pair of sparkling eyes. The look on her face was pride and Ken thought she looked beautiful.

Then Ken looked over at his dad. He saw a reaction that he could hardly believe; his father had tears in his eyes.

It hadn't occurred to Ken until that moment, what his progress in school had meant to his father and how important it was that his son did well in school. He vowed right then and there to make some changes. What a huge difference that moment in the car made in Kens life. He took on a new direction, striving to make his parents proud.

Already his personal interests in science were blossoming so he focused on nurturing his scholastic career and those efforts paid off. During his junior year he was voted Class President, he sat on the student council, he was a student member of PTA Steering committee, and Ken's Debate team won the NFL (National Forensic League) District Championship which included Nebraska and three adjacent states.

With a large dose of intelligence but only a half a serving of common sense at times, Ken landed himself in some pretty precarious predicaments during these formidable years in high school.

Although his efforts toward increasing his intelligence would be a successful journey, it certainly wouldn't discourage a healthy measure of mischief that would accompany him through high school and beyond.

Two Story Monstrosity

1962

Ken's relationship with his father influenced so many of his bold ventures throughout his youth. It didn't stop there. That torch of pride he developed so many years ago with his dad, carried over into his adulthood.

This was apparent as his North American House Moving business continued to plug along nicely, creating a substantial profit margin with the 'Ready-to-move-in' packages he developed. Ken purchased the houses, moved the homes to the lots, sometimes even built the foundations, and remodeled them after charging the home buyer one initial price.

During an afternoon auction, a large brick two-story duplex came up for sale while the auctioneer ranted about the size and difficulty in moving the building. He seemed to be convinced that no one could move the monstrosity and in the end it would be a demolition project.

The auctioneer did a pretty good job convincing the crowd because Ken was the first bidder and no one countered. He bought the thing for $400. Ken thought it was really a nice house.

"Have you ever moved anything like this?" The auctioneer asked Ken over the finalization of the paperwork.

"No. I haven't." He answered. "But I can do it. How tough could it be?" He promptly resold the house and arranged delivery to the buyer's lot for $12,000. This was his Golden Goose.

The duplex weighed more than 150 tons so Ken purchased a tremendous amount of supplies and equipment to tackle the great task. His existing carrying beams weren't nearly heavy enough for the job so he purchased steel from a used steelyard. Ken was a lousy welder but this project granted him plenty of practice. He picked up two 18 inch steel I-beams and put them side by side and welded them together creating a giant H-beam. It measured 13 inches wide, 18 inches high and 60 feet long.

In addition to the weight of the beams, Ken had to buy 200 pieces of new cribbing that consisted of wood blocks measuring six inches x six inches x six feet long. The only place he could find them at a reasonable price was at a sawmill north of town where they were cutting green cottonwoods. The pieces weighed almost 80 pounds each and were so wet that under the weight of the house water ran out of them. He also required a new set of dollies with two keels and eight wheels under each keel. Ken would have to engineer those as well.

He received a $6,000 deposit upfront on the house but by now he had spent every dime. The engineering involved in lifting the house without loosening the bricks was incredibly complicated. Ken had nowhere to go for advice, at least none that he could afford.

Eventually the crew fit the enormous beams under the foundation and started jacking up the house. It was so heavy that the 20 ton jacks compressed the cribs so that at full lift of 10 inches, the house only raised two inches. When the crew released the jacks, the cribs sprung back up only to compress again, giving the house another two inch lift. Eventually they got the house ready to move.

Ken received another $3,000 once the house was loaded and ready to roll. Again, he had most of that spent before he got the job to this point.

When he contacted the power and phone companies to move all of the wires, they charged Ken $1,800. Writing out the two checks, he seriously considered using John to move the wires for any future jobs because that was the last of the $3,000 he had coming upon completion.

The job was a financial disaster. Regardless, Ken felt a sense of accomplishment rather than defeat due to his engineering efforts. Some of the costs were offset by the reuseable heavy duty house moving equipment. More importantly he was proud of completing the job, on time, despite his many obstacles.

Ken was destined to repeat this sentiment for the rest of his life.

Barn Shocker

1962

After the two-story brick building disappointment, Ken dusted himself off and got back in the game. He decided to add barn moving to his repertoire when he agreed to relocate a barn for a gentleman in Irvington, Nebraska.

John showed up at the Bauer house early Monday morning ready to work, while Ken waited inside having breakfast with his family.

"Come on in, John." Ken shouted toward the knocking. The big man's footsteps announced his arrival.

"Mornin' Missa Kinny. Miz Alice."

"Morning John," Alice scooted a chair back with her foot for John to join them at the table, "coffee?"

"No thanks, Miz Alice, already had me some." John smiled at the two young boys sitting at the Bauer dining table drinking their chocolate milk. With five little Bauer's, their milkman stayed busy. He visited so often that he'd treat the kids to little pint cartons of chocolate milk once in a while. Both David and Marty were enjoying their treat this morning.

"You know," John scooted up closer to the table and said to the boys, "I see you sho does like that choclate milk."

"Mmmhmm" Marty said.

"You know, when eyez about yo age, maybe a little younger . . . eyez started drinkin dat choclate milk, too." David looked up from his milk to listen to John.

"Befo I started drinkn' it, eyez as white as you are. . . an look at me now!"

David's mouth flew open and he pushed the chocolate milk away. Marty laughed at John and took another drink. He finished David's drink, too, and David never drank chocolate milk again!

Ken and John laughed out loud; Alice rolled her eyes and continued with her crossword puzzle.

"Let's get going, John. We've got to get some measurements on that barn we're moving and we're meeting Al at the jobsite."

"Awhright, Missa Kinny."

On the drive to the barn site Ken explained his precarious situation. "This guy asked me to move his barn and when I drove the route to the new location –"

"Wherez dat?"

"In Irvington." John nodded his head.

"I came to that bridge over the Elkhorn River and when I measured the distance between the bridge rails, they were about 3 feet too narrow and about 7 feet high."

"An dat barn wont fit?"

"Nope. So I drove around looking for other routes across the river but they were even worse. So we gotta figure out a way to get across this bridge." Ken recognized the puzzled look on John's face. "What?"

"Well, if it don't fit, Missa Kinny, why you take the job?"

Ken explained that last week, after all of his research for alternate routes, he had called the people with the barn and spoke with Mrs. Kaufman.

"Boy, I'd really like to be able to move the barn for you but I can't get it over that bridge out there. It's about 3 feet too narrow," Ken explained to her.

"Oh, I am so sorry to hear that. We never even got to talk about a price - I was going to give you $5,000 to move that barn." After a moment of silence she added: "It's only 3 feet too wide, isn't there something you could do?"

Ken thought about her offer. In those days, $5,000 may as well have been a million. He concluded she was right – certainly he could think of some way to get her barn moved over that bridge.

He took the job. After all, how tough could it be?

Arriving on the site, Ken re-measured the height of the rail. While he was standing there trying to figure out a way to get this thing over this bridge, he thought maybe he could cut a slot in the barn and feed that bridge rail through the slot.

This would take some real structural engineering to make this work because the wall would fall off if it wasn't braced correctly. He ran several long 2x12 beams, like floor joists, ending just short of where he intended to cut the slot. At that point he braced the beams on the slot end up to the roof rafters. He then reinforced the joint where the hanging wall fit to the top plate of roof rafters. He calculated this was strong enough to hang there for the trip over the bridge.

After measuring the height of the barn, they discovered they were not going to clear the phone and power lines. From past experience Ken knew how terribly expensive this was going to be.

He decided that since this job was going to be out of city limits he allowed as how they could clear most of the wires and the ones that they couldn't, he would probably have enough slack in them to lift them over the barn. After all, they were out on quiet country roads. The barn cleared several miles of wires with no complications.

However, the first set of wires they encountered that required raising was a power drop that ran across the road down to a little farmhouse. Back in those days, the wires were coated with insulation that was vulnerable to the weather, leaving patchy places where the bare wire was exposed. This was a problem because if the bare spots touched each other, they would short out.

Ken stood in the middle of the road, looking up at four wires crossing the street like a limbo stick that his barn was going to have to crawl under. *Can I get enough stretch on those wires to clear it*? He wondered. He decided he would find a small tree branch with a "Y" on the end, something like he used as a kid for a sling shot crotch; he spotted one.

He pointed the tree out to John. "Can you climb up in that tree and cut that branch off there?" John scurried up into the tree and cut the limb off that Ken had pointed out. Ken stripped the bark off and instructed John to climb up onto the roof of the barn with his 'lifting stick'.

"Ahhwww I don't like dis," John said under his breath.

"Alright now, John," Ken shouted while John positioned himself high up on the barn roof, "were going to move ahead very slowly," Ken repositioned to the front of the truck so he could guide Al and still keep an eye on John. "…and these wires are to be kept apart.

"Now, the main thing that you have to remember is DO NOT TOUCH ANY OF 'EM TOGETHER – because if you do, ya know, it will flash and it will really hurt!" Ken watched John nod his head.

The heavy load crept forward with John on the roof of the barn with his wire lifting stick in position. The first thing he did was to lift the bottom wire and push all four of them up together.

SKKKZZZZZZZTTTTT!

Poor ol' John; he came sailing off of the roof. Ken raced over to find him lying in the ditch on his back, his eyes rolled back in his head and his mouth open. Ken thought for sure he had killed him!

"John? Are you all right?"

John opened one eye. "Missa Kinny . . . you needs to get somebody dats got skill for dis job."

Ken laughed with relief, "Oh, John! Did you break anything? You alright?"

"No, nuttn broke. I think eyez okay." Ken helped John to his feet and had him go rest in the shade.

While John recouped a while, Ken borrowed the telephone at the little farmhouse to call the electric company and get their power restored.

After he finished his calls, Ken walked back to check on his employee; he saw an old calico colored cat playing in the tall grasses over by John. Ken sat down next to his friend and told him a childhood story in the cool, quiet country shade.

Here Kitty Kitty

1947

It wasn't only war movies that inspired the two Nebraska twelve year olds. Once Ken and Donnie paid their dues for the foxhole mess and their parental ban on war movies was lifted, the twosome decided they were interested in Western's. Both of the youngsters envied the older boys and asked regularly for a rifle, to which they were regularly denied.

"Use your imagination." Ken's mother told him one afternoon following his father's rejection for the third time that month. Ken was getting nowhere quick with his parents on this subject.

What a good idea, mother! He finally thought to himself. Remembering their carved milk carton candle holders down in the fort, Ken figured there might be another use for them.

"We can build our own rifle!" Ken announced to Donnie.

"Yeah? How?"

"Remember when the cowboys were all bedded down around their campfire for the night and the bad guys came into the camp with guns?"

"Uhh huh."

"Remember when ol' Tom Mix reached into his pouch and pulled out a handful of bullets –

"… and then threw them into the fire?" an eager Donnie interrupted.

"Yeah, and the bullets exploded?!"

"Right!!" Donnie bubbled over with excitement. This was their favorite part of the movie for two reasons. First, it created a distraction for the cowboys to overcome and prevail and second, it fascinated the boys that ammunition could explode when exposed to fire.

"What are you thinking?" Donnie asked. Soon the boys agreed it was time for their first experiment out in Donnie's barn.

Donnie's father, Andrew kept an old yellow tomcat out in the barn. The scroungy feline had meandered onto the property months ago packing fleas' (mother was certain) along with an odious cats breath smelling of fishy curdled milk. He was more of a nuisance than a pet, of no particular value other than being a decent mouser, and his worst attribute was his insistent leg-rubbing. This desperate demand for affection resulted in mounds of yellow, parasite-infested fur left behind on your pant leg.

The boys pushed open the heavy door to the weathered two-story barn and looked around at their new workshop. Within seconds the ol' yella cat was rubbing up against Donnie sounding like a sputtering motor boat about to run out of gas. Donnie 'relocated' the mangy thing about two feet across the barn a couple of times with the side of his boot.

"Git outta here!" But the cat persisted. The third time the cat yowled and decided to head for higher ground, climbing up on top of a stack of empty fruit crates. This turned out to be a great spot for the tomcat to observe the goings on, while looking directly out the window where the boys would be working. Rejected, but out of the way of Donnie's leather boot heel, the cat busied himself with a sour-milk, sandpaper tongue bath.

Meanwhile, Donnie found a 4-foot length of rusted iron pipe. The boys lifted open the barn window and wedged the pipe through it, resting the heavy window back down on the pipe for support.

Next they rounded up an old .22 shell and placed it into the pipe. Ken brought along one of his milk cartons. He carved a piece of the carton so that the top would fit over the barrel of their new 'gun'. The idea was to put a candle in the carton, light it under the shell and the shell would ignite, shooting the bullet out the other end of the pipe like a gun barrel.

Outside of the barn the boys placed a large white pickle bucket on a stump. From within the barn they aimed the pipe at the bucket. Now it was time to light the candle.

They quietly watched the flame flicker inside of the milk carton, heating their .22 shell for a short time until it exploded. Fortunately, Donnie and Ken were positioned on either side of the 'gun'. The shell exploded and the cat let out a terrible shriek.

RRrrrrryyywwww!!! The boys realized they had shot the cat and the bullet had never left the barrel. The pipe was so big it didn't confine the shell jacket and when the shell exploded it blew jacket shrapnel backwards out of the pipe and killed the damn cat.

"Awwwhhh no, Ken! Now what are we gunna do?"

Ken thought for a moment. Although he was grateful that he and Donnie hadn't killed themselves, he couldn't stop thinking about the punishment this kind of trouble would earn them.

"Let's get rid of this gun. If they find out about this you and I will never see a rifle."

Donnie pulled an old gunny sack out from behind a pile of tires and scooped the tomcat inside. "Poor ol' sucker." Donnie said to the contents in the bag. "I sure didn't like him, but I never wanted something like that to happen to him."

"How 'bout we go bury him somewhere out in the yard?" Ken suggested, picking up the rest of the shrapnel from the dirt floor.

The boys tossed the pipe out on a burn pile and then proceeded to bury the cat under a peach tree.

"If my ol' man ever asks," Donnie said to Ken looking down at the mound of dirt, "we just tell him 'he musta run away'."

Both boys agreed on the tomcat alibi. They also decided that would be the end of their gun making business.

* * *

"Awwhhh, Missa Kinny. You sho was a lil' devil back in dem days." John laughed.

Now that he was feeling better, Ken got the barn rolling down the road again. The next obstacle was the bridge. Since most of the day had been wasted with slingshot fabrication and power restoration it was getting late in the evening and Ken got out of the truck to look at the bridge again. He realized he had made a horrible mistake.

There were actually telephone poles next to the bridge but only on the right side. The bridge rail on the left hand side was completely open. Ken had cut the holes on the wrong side of the barn. "Dammit!"

"What is it Missa Kinny, we gotsta move more wires? I don't think I'm up to doin' any mo today, Missa Kinny."

"No, no, John - I wouldn't do that to you again." Ken was thankful that John didn't get hurt badly.

Looking back and forth from the poles to the holes, Ken's frustration mounted. He was so mad at himself and he couldn't even blame John for this one. *If I'd hired an engineer I could fire the son of a bitch*, Ken thought – but this was entirely his fault.

Ken huddled the guys. "Here's what we got to do. We've got to back the son of a bitch over the bridge so that the rails go through the holes in the barn."

Al, Ken's black truck driver, was a hell of a driver. Unfortunately, he was also a hell of a drinker. Due to the late hour Ken decided to wait until tomorrow to back the barn across the bridge.

"Now, Al," Ken tells his driver, "it's really important to get across this bridge tomorrow and we have absolutely no wiggle room on this . . . absolutely no room for mistakes."

"Yes, Missa Kinny."

"God dammit, Al - if you drink tonight I'm guna kill ya, do you understand that?"

"Oh, yes – yes, I do Missa Kinny."

Bright and early the next morning, Ken and his crew were met at the bridge by a Highway Patrolman. He stopped by to watch them move the barn and stop traffic. Now, Ken is not a religious man, but he prayed that his threat had gotten through to his driver the night before.

He watched Al drive the barn out a ways from the bridge, turn it around, and line the hole he had cut in the barn up with the left hand guard rail.

It was a cold Nebraska morning so Al had the windows rolled up in the truck. Ken wanted to make sure he was competent to back the barn over the bridge so he climbed up on to the running board to talk to Al. Ken motioned for him to roll the window down.

Wwhewwww, the smell of alcohol wafted out of the cab and nearly knocked Ken backwards off his truck!

"God dammit, Al! I told you not to do no drinkin'!"

"I didn't drink much, Missa Kinny."

"Holy shit, Al" Ken was trying to keep his voice down, "you gotta back this thing over this bridge."

"I think I can back it up alright. Don't u worry none."

"You keep these Goddammed windows down, you hear me? Air this cab out." Ken jumped down off of the truck, shaking his head knowing full well backing this barn over the bridge was going to be incredibly difficult. If Al made a mistake, it would spell disaster.

Out of his peripheral, Ken watched the Highway patrolman while he guided Al this way, that way, then a little bit the other way with only a small space on either side. He was hoping to avoid any unnecessary attention to the balancing act on their skinny bridge.

Inch by careful inch, the tires tiptoed over the wooden bridge and Ken let out a sigh of relief when the barn made it to the other side. The Highway Patrolman drove across the bridge to join them.

"Mr. Bauer, I'm going to have to talk to that truck driver of yours." Ken said nothing. Instead, he watched the patrolman walk to the truck and step up to Al's window.

Fuck! We're all going to jail! This thought repeated in Ken's head.

Al didn't move – he stared straight ahead reading Ken's mind. Finally, his bloodshot eyeballs creeped to the left corners of his eyes while his head slowly followed and he looked right at the officer.

The man took off his glasses. "I want to shake your hand, sir." He extended his hand through the window to Al. "That was some of the finest driving I've ever seen in my life." He said shaking Al's hand.

Ken breathed his second biggest sigh of relief for that day. He couldn't wait to get the building turned around again and set on Kaufman's property.

Bolts & Bulldozers

1962

Ken developed several techniques while learning the ins and outs of the house moving business. While in Duluth, he moved relatively light houses after acquiring a basic rudimentary procedure. It became whole different ball game moving houses in the urban Omaha environment; not to mention the fact that Ken upped the ante by tackling larger, heavier homes.

Recognizing the importance to further his knowledge, and satisfying his curiosity, Ken searched for 'how to' books on house moving. Unfortunately, no such book existed or if it did, he couldn't find it. He observed his competitors to gain new insights, gleaning a few ideas from them and ultimately engineering new apparatus's and formulating techniques to compliment this new equipment.

One thing had become glaringly constant in Ken's life: Whenever there was a little trouble on the job, John was close at hand!

Shortly after Ken hired John, he devised a system to clamp large I-beams together. It involved one inch steel plates tied together with four 1¼ inch threaded steel bolts with enormous nuts. Tightening them involved a 36-inch pipe wrench accompanied by a six foot piece of two inch steel pipe for leverage.

Ken decided this would be a good task for the brawny man, given his considerable strength. One particular afternoon the crew prepared to move a house to a lot on the South side of Omaha.

"John," Ken hollered, "why don't you go put those plates on the bunk out there and tighten them up like I showed you." Knowing how strong he was, he added: "You won't need to use that cheater."

"Okay, Missa Kinny. I'll tighten it right up for ya."

Ken disappeared into the basement of the house. Before long he could hear the bolts squeaking as John tightened them. Another employee, Dick Stimpson, happened to be working side-by-side with Ken down in the basement. Dick looked up in the direction of the whining metal.

CRrrreeeeeeeek. . . CRrrreeeeeeeek

"Ken," Dick looked over at his boss, "sounds like he's getting those bolts awful tight."

Ken stopped what he was doing and hollered up at John, "You ain't usin' that cheater bar, are you?"

"No suh, Missa Kinney, I jus got dis wrench."

Dick and Ken listen to the metal creek a couple more times.

BANG! John snapped a steel bolt.

Ken could hardly believe anyone could break off one of those huge bolts by hand. Of course there were no spares available so another one had to be built.

* * *

Ken bid another job requiring a house to be placed into a hillside. First a hole was dug into the hillside, then the house was backed into the hole, and then it had to be jacked up to foundation height. Once the dwelling was backed into the hole, Ken left John and Al to jack the house up into position.

"Now when you guys jack this thing up, be really careful that you don't lay this cribbing parallel on top of each other." He pointed out to the guys before leaving for his office across town. "Make sure to build a square crib because otherwise it could roll."

Ken arrived at his office by noon, ate lunch and started in on some paperwork. Around 3 o'clock in the afternoon he received a call from John.

"Uhhh, Missa Kinny, we done had little trouble on the job."

Ken throws his pen down on his desk.

"Jesus, John! What'd you do now?"

"It wuddn't my fault, Missa Kinny . . . Al told me to go ahead 'n just stack dem things up straight, one piece on topa da other, an I knew dat wasn't right, but Al said it'd be a lot faster thata way.

"And he was right, Missa Kinny. It went fast. Sep, we stack 'em up dat way and dat damn house acted like it was guna start rollin' foward all by itself!"

Ken sat with both elbows on his desk; one hand held the telephone to his ear and the other hand supported his forehead rubbing his temples with his thumb and fingers. He felt the raging tidal wave of a headache coming on.

"...so we start scampering out from underneath there, so it don't fall on us!" John reports, "but that ol' house fell right down an crashed into da bottom of dat hole."

"Oh my aching ass!"

Ken sent the boys home after the conversation with John.

Returning to the site the next morning, headache free, Ken discovered part of the situation was due to the construction taking place on the lot up above and behind them. He watched a D10-Cat operator bulldoze the lot above the house, preparing it for a building pad. The vibration from the heavy piece of equipment may have contributed to the accident.

Ken turned his attention back to his own job site and got Al and John started on lifting the house back up and reconstructing the cribs correctly. Recognizing that the impact of the crashing house caused spider web cracks all throughout the plaster, he knew this was going to cost him more to fix than what he earned for the job.

"John, why don't you go park that winch truck somewhere else so it's not in our way." He instructed him. John moved the truck to the far side of the house, up against the bank where the new pad was under construction.

Once again Ken reached a point of confidence with his guys and he drove back to the office to bid on plans for other jobs. Like clockwork, in the middle of the afternoon, the phone rang and it was John.

"Uhh, Missa Kinny, we done had little trouble on da job."

"Oh, Jesus Christ, John! What'd you do this time?"

"It wuddn't my fault, Missa Kinny . . . you know dat winch truck you use ta have?"

Oh shit!

"Well, you know dat man wid da great big bulldozer up on topa dat bank?

"Yeah?"

"You member you had me park dat winch truck over outta da way next to da bank?"

"Yeah?"

"Well, he done backed dat dozer right over da topa yo winch truck. Smashed it down flat as a pancake –"

Ken groaned into the phone line.

". . .it ain't but maybe 3 feet high!" John reported.

Although the Cat operator's insurance company bought the North American Moving Company another used winch truck, the massive plaster repair made the job a huge looser.

A few days later Ken was finally able to laugh about the situation. John was retelling the story again and Ken couldn't help but chuckle.

"When dat dozer squished yo winch truck, it made da biggest clouda dust you eva saw Missa Kinny." For some reason that reminded Ken of his high school days and the time he scared the bejeezus out of the janitor.

Purple Haze of High School

1952

Sixteen year old Kenneth miraculously survived his junior year in Bauer explosives 101! Preserving all of his body parts, his friends, family, and home – he successfully entered his senior year at Omaha Technical High School. Ken had come up with a great idea for his required senior project!

Ken approached Mr. Dubler one afternoon. "Can I surprise you with my senior project?"

"Well, if it's going to be a surprise," he considered the request, "it had better be a good one."

By now Ken had discovered how to make all different kinds of explosives from nitroglycerin and dynamite to even more powerful explosives. His last experiment happened over the summer when he developed a fondness for Nitrocellulose (gun cotton) and Picric Acid (the explosive used in the war heads of Naval shells).

The Picric Acid contains water of crystallization so it has to be melted and cast into a block to become an explosive. Ken came up with one of his brilliant ideas to use his dad's dark room print dryer to melt the explosive because it has such an even heat. Unfortunately, it was located right under his dad's enlarger. So when it finally melted, it flashed so quickly that it burned up the print dryer, scorched the enlarger, and took off both of Ken's eyebrows!

In another experiment, he learned how to take gun cotton and mix it with nitroglycerin, dissolve it in alcohol, turning it to a gel state that was perfect for a blasting gelatin.

All kinds of shapes could be created from this gelatin. Then it could be used as shape charges to blow holes in things.

Also, he discovered he could nitrate starch, turning it into granite, which was used in hand grenades. And all of these adventures ultimately led him to the innocent, yet spectacular discovery of Ammonium iodide.

One day while Ken and Mr. Dubler discussed explosives, the Teacher recounted some of his years in college.

"You know, we did something in college chemistry." Pausing, the teacher reconsidered making such an admission, "…nahhhh, I'd better not tell you. You'll go off and be making this stuff."

"No – I won't make it! I promise. What was it?"

"Well, it was an explosive called ammonium iodide. It was really amazing because it formed these little purple crystals."

Ken hung on every word, nodding and listening, and dreaming of Chinese fireworks again! The teacher continued.

"Now, when these crystals were wet, they wouldn't explode, but the minute they dried – the slightest vibration would set them off. My gosh, if the wind would blow over the top of them, or someone stepped on them, man they would go off! Now, the really neat thing was - when they did explode, you would have this little purple atomic bomb cloud."

Ohhhhhh, man! Ken's eyes filled with various hues of Northern Lights! He just had to make some of that. So he asked Mr. Dubler how they made it.

"You promise you won't make it?"

"Oh yeah!" Ken promised. "I won't make it." Ken bit down hard on his bottom lip in order to contain his bubbling enthusiasm.

"Well, what you do is to take concentrated reagent grade ammonium hydroxide, mix in iodine crystals and you have ammonium iodide."

Ken was happier than a fat kid hiding cake under his pillow. After school, he found himself back in the chemical room with his beaker - brewing up purple hopes and dreams. There he stood mixing ammonia and iodine crystals with no idea of what ratios to use.

Ken started by filling a beaker half full of ammonia and dumping a couple of spoons full of the crystals into the beaker. Then he placed it under the vacuum hood, reached under and stirred it, and the stuff turned purple. But crystals didn't dissolve.

Humm? He wasn't sure how to proceed.

He considered that maybe he dumped too many crystals into the ammonia. Ken looked around and located some filter paper, dumped the mixture through and filtered out the excess crystals; pitching those into the waste basket.

Now he had a purple liquid. He placed his purple concoction under the vacuum to dry it out and harvest the crystals. But once it dried up, he was left with nothing, nothing but disappointment. No action or reaction.

He was bullshitting me, Ken thought. *Mr. Dubler just wanted to see if I'd try to make it*. Feeling a bit foolish and defeated, Ken cleaned up his experiment and left the room. He passed the janitor on the way down the hallway.

"Hello." Ken said to the man pushing a large garbage bin on wheels.

"Hello, son." The janitor replied on his way in to empty the wastepaper baskets from the chemical room.

Lost in his thoughts Ken continued down the hallway. No sooner than he turned the corner at the end of the hallway, he heard: *BABOOOM!*

Ken stopped dead in his tracks and turned to go look around the corner. Purple smoke clouds billowed out into the hallway, tumbling over themselves! *Oh God, I killed the janitor!*

Ken started breathing again once he heard the man holler, "What the hell?!"

Now only one thought raced through his head: *ALRIGHT! I did learn how to make it! I just threw away the wrong stuff!*

It seemed that his lessons in explosives had now fully matured, at least to a point where the 'purple boom' would become the 'cherry' on top of his secret senior project!

On the day the Senior Projects were due, Ken showed up at school with several samples of high explosives, carefully placed in a wooden fruit lug. When it was finally his turn he set up all of his samples on the table, opened the windows to let out any smoke, and started his demonstration.

He got lots of *oooohhh's* and *ahhhhh's* when he lit his gunpowder to show how it burned fast and then how it would explode when contained.

Then Ken explained about which things needed detonators and why, making other small explosions to keep his audience interested. It wasn't too far into his presentation before the principal showed up to watch the show. He took a seat on one of the wide window sills and watched the young chemist while he put on quite a show with his samples of high explosives.

After class was over, the principal pulled Ken aside to applaud his efforts.

"You did a wonderful job, Kenneth; that was quite a demonstration. You take the rest of the afternoon off," he calmly said, patting him on the back, "and get this stuff the hell out of my building."

Best Christmas Ever!

1962

Ken's North American House Moving business was running around Omaha wearing a tourniquet. Despite his best efforts, money was short for everyone during the holidays and the twenty-eight year old entrepreneur desperately wanted to give the two men on his crew a Christmas bonus.

Several days before Christmas, Ken devised a plan to get everyone trees because that was another luxury no one could afford. There just so happened to be an empty lot they had recently moved a house from and it was scheduled to be cleared and leveled for building after the holidays. This lot happened to have several large pine trees. Ken rounded up Al one early morning before life was stirring and headed over to the job site.

"Al," Ken said to his faithful employee while sitting in the heated cab of the pickup, "what do you say about climbing up into that tree over there and sawing the top off to make us a Christmas tree?"

Al leaned over his steering wheel and looked up at the giant pine spotlighted by the headlights.

"I suppose dat wouldn' be too hard." Al stared at the tree.

"Well OK!" Ken attempted some enthusiasm and opened the passenger door to go and retrieve a hand saw from the back of the pickup. Al followed suit and opened his door letting the rest of the winter chill fill the cab of the truck. From the bed of the truck Ken handed Al the saw.

"So, you a wantn' me to climb up in that ol' pine tree and cut it, den let it fall to da groun?" Al had the saw in his hand while still staring at the tree.

"Yup." Ken answered. He was feeling the festive spirit now. Al, John, and Ken's families would all have nice, big evergreen Christmas trees!

Ken placed both hands on the side of the truck bed and gingerly swung both legs over to land on the ground next to Al. Away they went to harvest them some Christmas trees.

Al climbed up into three different trees; lopping off around 6 feet of the tops and watching them fall another 20 feet to the ground. Once they were all on the ground, Ken's spirits dampened a bit. Frowning at the tree tops in front of him he decided they were going to take a bit of work.

"Aren't those the damndest things you ever saw?" Ken asked. Al stood one of the three amputees up and slowly spun it to examine more closely. They both stared at the big gaps between the branches.

"I got an idea." Ken said and he asked Al to keep a hold of the tree. "When you and John get these tree's home, you chop off a few of these lower branches. Then you take a drill, make some holes in these bare spots," Ken was pointing to the bald spots in the tree, "and sharpen the ends of the branches to stick them in the holes. You'll have a beautiful looking Christmas tree." Ken already knew that Alice would work her magic on their pitiful looking tree and make it incredibly beautiful just as she had every year since they were married.

Although Ken knew the trees were a nice gesture, he still wanted to come up with a gift for his employees and their families. Not having the funds put him into quite a holiday funk.

Then on Christmas morning, his friend Lee called to offer both holiday cheer and a solution to his problem.

"Hey Ken, Merry Christmas!" Lee's enthusiastic voice percolated through the line as Ken stood in his living room with his phone up to his ear, "I think I know what you can do for John and Al for a Christmas present."

"Oh yeah, what's that?"

"I saw a newspaper ad where a farmer has some geese he's selling for a buck apiece."

Ken thought about this as Lee continued. "You could get 'em both a goose for dinner." Ken smiled, looking out his large picture window at the ground that sparkled white as far as his eye could see.

"Oh, yeah." Ken replied. "That would be super!"

Ken met Lee at his house and the two drove to the farm together. As they made their way up the long twisting driveway, they passed a couple of waddling geese a few hundred feet from the farmhouse.

"Those are the biggest damn geese I've ever saw!" Lee said to Ken, looking over the back seat; watching them get smaller though the back window of Ken's Chevy station wagon.

Ken pulled the vehicle up near a path that lead to the farmer's porch and the two men stepped out of the car, not realizing their feathered friends had followed them up the drive. Lee happened to look over his shoulder and from opposite sides of the farm yard, the two geese had their long necks stretched out parallel with the ground, beaks snapping, wings unfurled and they were picking up speed in a full charge headed straight for them.

Ken looked over at Lee; his eyes had enlarged to the size of golf balls.

"Run, Kenny – RUN!" Lee hollered. Ken looked back to see the crazed birds charging right for them. They had just enough time to get to the enclosed porch where someone was already waiting.

The farmer may as well have been Santa himself incognito, except for his countrified attire. Laughing, the man kicked the rickety screen door. "Gwone. Get outta here!" He scolded the geese, and they surprisingly obeyed him like well trained guard dogs, waddling off somewhere to mingle with the other loose geese meandering around the farm.

The man turned to the panting strangers on his porch. He was dressed in denim overhauls that stretched taut over his large belly, muddied goulashes, and an old, frayed Caterpillar baseball cap that appeared to be holding down an unruly mane of thick, grey hair.

"Uh, Hello," Ken extended his right hand.

"Hello." The farmer returned a firm handshake to Ken, and then to Lee.

"I understand that you have some geese for sale for a dollar." Ken asked the man.

"Yes sir, I have." He replied, and opened the screen door to lurch his chin forward and spit a mouthful of chaw onto the ground.

"I suppose that you have 'em already killed and plucked?" Ken asked.

The man wiped the chaw drool from his bearded chin with the back of his hand. It had already started to freeze and some of the brown goo remained behind, safely clinging to the gray strands.

Country Santa's belly began to shake in response to Ken's question. "No sir." He laughed. "That's why I'm sellin' 'em for a dollar. They're like pets," he continued, "but they're so goddamned aggressive and downright mean." The man paused to look at the latest victims. "They chase anyone that comes in the yard. I've gotta get rid of 'em. It's like havin' a mean dog. So that's why I'm sellin' 'em for a buck."

Ken and Lee looked at one another, and then Ken turned back to the farmer. "Well, what do I have to do? Shoot them?"

"No, no." He said. "Don't do that, not in front of me. I've got some feed sacks over here," and he turned to a pile of burlap draped over an old wooden rocker there on his porch. "You can catch 'em and put 'em in these feed sacks." He said handing a couple of the scratchy fabric bags to Ken.

Once again, Ken and Lee looked at one another. Ken shrugged and said, "How tough can it be?"

So the Jolly farmer explained that Ken could buy as many as he could catch.

"I only need a couple." Ken told him.

The city slickers allowed as how they needed a plan. Ken and Lee peered out at the freakishly large, angry geese that were busy pecking grain from the frozen ground at the far end of the yard. The big man watched Ken and Lee for a moment, and his big belly began to convulse once more in riotous laughter.

Lee stood looking at the birds. He began to nod his head up and down. "Sooo, we just . . . corner one of them . .

. and . . . throw him in the bag, right?" He was desperately looking for confirmation from the farmer. He didn't get any.

After a moment of silence, Ken said, "Well, let's go." So the farmer swung open his front porch screen and into the goose arena they went.

They could see the geese several yards ahead of them. Ken threw one sack on the ground and opened the end of the other, still unsure of what to do next.

"Uh, oh," Lee says, "we got a problem. Looks like that son-of-a-bitch is headed straight at us!" A large goose had put his head down and was preparing to charge!

"Ok." Ken said, not taking his eyes off the goose. "Let's do like a matador: each of us stepping to one side - and we'll grab him on the way by."

So they took hold of the burlap and the goose charged through the sack like a mad bull. Lee stepped aside and let go of the bag. Ken was able to get one hand around the goose's neck just before the giant fowl drug him to the ground and proceeded to beat the living be-geezus out of him with his wings!

"Get the damn sack, Lee!" Ken hollered between beatings. But the giant wings of Lucifer flapped, and flapped and nearly beat Ken to death before Lee could get a hold of the goose to try and stuff him into the sack.

Ken escaped the entangled battle long enough to grab a webbed foot, as Lee managed to fold a wing down, and the two slickers wrestled the damn creature into a burlap bag. Ken ended up with a bloodied lip and thumps and bumps all up and down his arms and all over his head. He was certain many of them were going to develop into large bruises; and what John would later refer to as 'Missa Kinny's Goose Eggs'.

Ken and Lee finally got the angry goose stuffed down in the bag. Like a couple of professional hog-tiers, round and round they wrapped the twine until the top of the bag was tightly secured.

"This is one pissed off goose!" Lee said, out of breath.

"Don't you know it." Ken said to Lee who was nearly sitting on the bagged goose to keep him still. "One more to go."

"What? Awhh, shit, Ken." Lee looked like a rodeo clown bouncing up a bit every time the goose squawked and wriggled in the bag.

"Well, this was your brilliant idea!" Ken reminded him.

So, the two city slickers went through it again while the farmer stood there on his porch and laughed out loud. They proudly materialized from the arena with two giant, angry, Christmas geese in bags. Ken paid his two dollars to the man, realizing this entire ordeal was designed for the farmer's entertainment.

The two exhausted warriors headed for their car; the sound of Country Santa's laughter still lingering in the winter air behind them.

"What you suppose John and Al are gunna do with these birds?" Ken asked his friend, loading the geese into the back of the car.

The birds flopped around in their bags on the deck of the station wagon. "I suppose they'll clean 'em and cook 'em up." Lee said. And off the two went to John's house for the first goose delivery.

* * *

"Merry Christmas!" Ken said to John's six year old son when he answered the door. The little boy stared up at Ken, looked down at the bag, then back at Ken before answering him. Finally he managed a weak and somewhat concerned reply.

"Merry Christmas, Missa Kinny."

"Where's John?" Ken asked, trying to hold steady the crazy bag of unknown behind his back. Lee stood quietly behind Ken, uncertain of what else this National Lampoon's Christmas adventure could possibly turn into.

"Daddy still in bed dis mornin'."

"He is?" Ken asked as the devil horns slowly began to protrude above each of his temples. *Well, isn't that just perfect!* He thought to himself.

"Yas sir. But you come on in here Missa Kinny cuz Daddy'll wana see ya." John's son opened the door wide so the two men and the unknown bag of wriggle and squawk could pass. Ken walked through the front door and realized that the bedroom door was right off of the living room - making his plan even more convenient.

Jr. hoped back on his couch, flopping his little brown arms over the back, watching to see what Missy Kinny was going to do with that bag of commotion.

Ken reached the bedroom door, grabbed hold of the door knob, slowly opened the door enough to get the bag inside and he shook that damn goose loose into poor John's bedroom.

"Merry Christmas, John!" Ken shouts.

Honk! Honk! They hear the goose running around flapping his giant angry wings. The next thing Ken, Lee and Jr. heard was an angrier sound coming from John's wife –

"John, you get dat goddamn goose outta here right now!" Mrs. John was shouting and banging against the walls, "Git 'im outta here, look at what he's gettin' into!"

"Git 'im outta here?" John shouted back at his wife. "What you mean?"

Honk, Honk!

"I ain't got no clothes on!" John hollered, "and he's a headn right tword me!"

Ken and Lee rolled around on John's hardwood floor in laughter. Jr. jumped up and down, squealing as loud as the goose. Little John Jr. was delighted with the Christmas cheer Missa Kinny done brung!

Ken and Lee decided that was so much fun that they headed over to Al's house. Only this time, they opened the front door to Al's place and shook the goose loose in the living room.

The whole house exploded in chaos as Al, his ol' lady, and the kids flew around trying to stay out of the way of the goose.

That turned out to be the funnest Christmas Ken & Lee had ever had.

Merry Christmas to all ~
. . . and to all a Good Night!

No Way Around It

1963

Over the years Ken had grown accustomed to dealing with angry authority figures and it seemed he'd been getting a tremendous amount of practice lately with his house moving business. However, one of the distractions that kept Ken in a great mood was planning for the annual springtime fishing trip to Kenora, Canada with Donnie Wilson.

They discovered that when you're broke planning for an adventure takes a little time. So they started every winter before the spring trip to throw an extra can of beans or box of crackers in the cart at the grocery store and after several months they would have their Kenora stockpile. Occasionally they would also stop at a sporting goods store to buy a lure that would be set aside especially for that occasion.

The plan was to drive to Canada over Memorial Day weekend. Unfortunately, Ken had run into a few wrinkles when he found himself right in the middle of moving a house located in Bellevue. This particular house had a rock face with all sorts of odd shaped stones adorning the front. When Ken went to move the house, he hadn't taken into consideration the weight in lifting all that stone.

After getting on the road much later than expected, all Ken thought about was how he was going to get the house delivered to a lot in Omaha in time to leave for Canada the next day.

He figured there was sufficient daylight to get the house moved to the lot and positioned over the hole where it belonged and then John and Al could jack the thing up, remove the dollies and prepare it for the block layers. It was the perfect plan. The only hiccup so far was the man with the maple tree who had a branch hanging over the street.

Ken knocked several times on the man's door but no one answered. Being on such a tight schedule he decided to have John climb up in the tree and cut the branch off. Halfway through cutting the branch, a man in a plaid bathrobe wandered out of his house. He was angry, mean as a junkyard dog, and had a shotgun in hand. He threatened to shoot John.

"Get out of that tree!" he hollered up to the large black man shaded under the maple leaves.

"Whoaa, heyyy Missa," John said holding up both of his hands. "Eyez jus cuttn dis branch off so Missa Kinny don't run dat house into it." John pointed with the saw. The man looked to see the wide load sitting a ways back down the road.

Ken straightened everything out with the armed Maple tree lover and the crew headed down 13th Street which turned into Highway 73: a very well traveled four-lane thoroughfare that connected Omaha to Offutt Air force base.

So far so good . . . I'll be fishing in no time, Ken daydreamed. He and the crew slowly made their way down the highway with their very heavy house until the truck lurched forward and stopped.

Ken discovered that the weight of the house had broken the axle on one of the dollies. He had used single dollies rather than a set of tandems not accounting for the additional weight of the stone.

Dammit!

Unable to move any further, Ken accepted the fact that they were stuck on 13th Street. They were in an area that looked down over Riverview Park, with a broken dolly.

Ken wandered around in the street trying to figure out what to do. He looked at his watch. It was nearly 6 p.m. and he had to leave for Canada the next morning. He allowed as how he would have to leave the house in the middle of the road. He saw no other way around the situation.

"John here's what we're going to do -"

Ken outlined a plan involving John and a 24-hour roadside service of flares. Back in those days, flares looked like some kind of cartoon Acme bomb that the Road Runner might use on Wiley coyote. The round, black objects came with a wick and could be re-filled with fuel oil which burned for several hours. These were the warning flares Ken instructed John to use.

"While I'm gone," he said to John, "I need you to come down here and fill up all of these flares every day and fill them again in the evening so that they burn all night long. You got that, John?"

"Okay Missa Kinny. I sho take care of it."

The next morning, Donnie and Ken headed for Kenora. In their excitement; Ken appeared only slightly concerned about having a giant house in the middle of a main street. It was possible there could be some consternation with the powers that be, especially considering his house was blocking the main access route to Offutt Air Force Base, but Ken felt confident in his man John. As the day progressed, he felt even more confident about the mess of fish he would be catching soon.

While Donnie and Ken escaped to enjoy a Canadian fishing trip, John spent one hell of a weekend down on 13th St.

Ken returned from Canada refreshed and ready to face the house he'd left in the middle of the road. Arriving at the site early Tuesday morning, John was all worked up. He couldn't wait to tell Ken about the events that transpired while he was gone.

"Missa Kinny, don't you never tell me do nuthin' like dat again." John said to Ken before he even had time to shut his car door. "If you needn' to leave, don't you dare volve me no more!"

"Why? What happened, John?" They both walked in the cool morning air toward the house.

"You told me come fill up those damn flares every night an I did. Eyez out there fillin' up dem flares an all of a sudden I sees dis car aheaden' straight for dat house. An I'll be Goddammed, dat man done turn to da right an drove right off that cliff down into Riverview Park!" Ken stopped to look at John considering the steep embankment leading from 13th Street overlooking the park that was full of trees and weeds.

"Was he alright?" Ken asked.

"Oh, yeah," John answered, "but he come up outta dare an he's mad as hell. Says he wants ta try 'n whip my ass."

Ken stifled his laughter, "Well, that would've been a poor choice." Ken said. John nodded.

Ken listened to John go on and on with his story – he was pretty worked up. The two of them walked around the house while Ken considered how to remove the broken dolly and weld the axle back together. He had to get this house moved to its location before any further trouble ensued.

Ken had his head up under the house and he could still hear John's voice.

"…and all dem people come up 'n honkn' at me every time I was here. I knowd there was nuthn' you could do all da way up 'n Canada. But I didn't like bein' da one in charge. I wuz always da bad guy wid that God damn house right in their way!"

Ken and his crew eventually fixed the dolly and got the house moved into its final destination.

Appeasing the folks from the police department and the city took Ken a little bit longer. Of course he apologized profusely and promised that he would never do something like that again, but he had stirred up quite a hornet's nest. Now his main concern was when he was going to get stung.

Down in the Dumps

1963

Ken eventually went broke in the house moving business. After that, he did his best to scrounge up other work for John. At one point Ken asked his father if he could use John on some of his jobs; Joe Bauer had a small business sweeping parking lots at night and he agreed to put John to work. Ken thought it best to remind his dad of a few things about his new employee.

While he stood in his driveway talking to his father through the driver side window, Ken attempted to warn him about John's strength.

"Just last week Tate was going to move his fish shop and I sent John over there to help him move some of those big expensive glass tanks." Tate owned the local tropical fish store and he and Ken had become good friends over the years.

"I told him, 'Whatever you do Tate, don't let him handle anything delicate. He has no idea how strong he is.

"He didn't even hear me, he says, 'Oh yeah, Ken I know, but that would be great to have John help me move some of these things.' So off John goes to help him out for the day."

"Sure enough I got a call later that night after they got everything moved and I asked Tate how John worked out for him.

"Tate says to me, 'well it started out the very first thing in the morning, I had my panel truck locked up and I sent John out there to put the first tank in it and he walked up to the door and twisted the handle clean off.'" Father and son laughed; their breath escaping as puffs of vapor into the cool, dark morning air. Ken continued with his story.

"Tate says, 'I looked out the window and there's John holding that handle in his hand!'

"Then Tate says 'it went on like that for the rest of the day.' He says, 'I was stupid enough to hand 'm that big neon sign, it's heavy as hell, but ol' John, he picked it up and crushed it like a cracker!'"

Both men snickered at John's expense there in the driveway. The dawn broke through the clouds and Ken's father flipped his visor down to shield his eyes. "Seriously dad, John's a really good worker but don't give him anything delicate to handle because he'll break it." John couldn't help himself - he was a bull in a china closet.

"Awhh, Kenny," his father shook his head, smiling down at his steering wheel, "I've heard all those stories before." Joe was certain that his son embellished most all of them. "Go ahead and send John over late this afternoon," he started the engine, "I have a couple of things I can have him do for me."

* * *

After Joe Bauer finished sweeping each parking lot, he dumped the sweeper out onto the ground and then shoveled the dirt into the back of his pickup. Normally he would head out to the dump site before dawn and unload the dirt out over the edge. This time he sent John out to what they referred to as the Canyon.

On the way to the dump, John heard the mournful cry of the groundskeeper's peacocks. They belonged to the couple who ran the dump and lived in a small home just past the entrance. It was shortly after dawn when Ken received a phone call.

"Missa Kinny, I done had little trouble on the job." He told Ken from the phone at the groundskeepers house.

"Jesus Christ, John! What'd you do this time?"

"It wuddn't my fault, Missa Kinny . . ." John launched into a long-winded explanation that started in Joe's driveway! He reached the end of the story just as Ken was reaching the end of his patience.

"…and I'm backn up your daddys truck down into the dump and there it still is."

"Well drive it out for Christ sakes."

"Well," John paused, "I cai'nt."

"Why not?"

"Cuz its way down in dat damn canyon there."

Ken closed his eyes and loosened the grip from around the telephone. He filled his lungs with air and slowly asked John, "How . . . did it get in the canyon, John?"

"I don't know. Eyez just bakn' it up . . . an it was dark . . . an the first thing I know, eyez down in da bottom of dat canyon. An I didn't know howda git it out."

Ken asked John to put the groundskeeper on the line. He made arrangements to come get his father's pickup and then requested that he put John back on the line.

"Just stay put, I'll be there soon as I can." He tells John.

Ken slipped on some gloves and a coat and hurried out the back door to fire up his winch truck. Arriving at the dump, Ken looked around for John but he was nowhere to be found.

He spotted the pickup down in the canyon. Ken parked in a safe spot, set the brakes and jumped out to unwind the winch from the back of the truck. The gravel and dry brush slipped beneath his feet as he made his way down the steep embankment. There at the bottom of the canyon dump was John, hiding behind the motionless vehicle.

"What are you doing, John?"

John poked his head around the corner of the truck. "Eyez afraid yo daddy maybe comen'. I didn't wants to have him see his truck down here in da bottom a dis canyon. Eyez afraid he might kill me."

Ken winched his dad's pickup from the bottom of the canyon. Surprisingly, it didn't appear to have any damage considering the mishap. Ken sent John on his way and opted not to mention anything to his father, knowing he could save the 'I told you so" for another day.

Earning Your Stripes

1964

Ken went to work for Paul Farnsworth, owner of a parking lot striping and seal coating business. Paul worked with Ken for several months teaching him the trade. Eventually, Ken became responsible for overseeing the seal coating operation. He also became the company salesman, responsible for fielding incoming calls and bidding jobs. The two of them even built a tennis court together for the Navy at Fort Omaha.

One morning a call came in from a large processed animal feed manufacturer and they wanted to build a new parking lot. Ken was interested, Paul was not.

"We could really make a lot of money on this, Paul." Ken tried to convince his boss. "If you would let me bid this and get the job, I know it would be good for both of us."

"I don't screw around building parking lots." Paul insisted. "We're not in that business - were in the striping and seal coating business and that's where I want to stay."

"Right Paul, but think about the Navy tennis court. Man, we knew absolutely nothing about building tennis courts at the time. We learned, did a beautiful job, and made a lot of money."

"Yeah, but that was more like the seal coating business."

Ken nodded in agreement, but he was still confident in his abilities and could see the potential of building these parking lots. All his life he had ventured into unchartered waters and was able to successfully reinvent himself. This was another one of those golden opportunities to spread his wings. Unfortunately, he could see that Paul had no interest in joining him on this adventure.

"Alright, Paul, but let me ask you this - would you be angry if Lee Anderson and I bid the job?"

"No." Paul compromised. "You go right on ahead if you want to."

Ken talked to Lee about the opportunity.

"I'm not in the parking lot business, Ken. I'm in the house building business." Lee stared at Ken and shook his head. "Are you nuts? We don't know anything about building parking lots."

"Oh, come on – how tough could it be?" Ken argued. "Besides, I know we could make a lot of money on this, Lee." Ken convinced his friend to allow him to place a bid and see what happened. As luck would have it, they were awarded the bid and were about to try their hands in the paving business. Ken made all of the arrangements, including discussing the specifics of the upcoming job with a representative at the plant.

To figure the bid, Ken pulled many of the specifications from a prior bid on the tennis court he and Paul worked on together. They landed that government job with the help of Chevron Asphalt Company. Ken figured if he used some of the same jargon, he would win this bid. The gamble worked.

"Hello. Yes, this is Ken Bauer with Anderson Paving and Construction." Both Ken and Lee decided to omit the Bauer name after going broke in the house moving business; his credit was shot. But as an experienced, salaried employee, Ken was able to get credit and maneuver until they established their company.

"I see here in your bid, Mr. Bauer that you plan to build the lot with a layer of rock, uh," the voice on the other end of the line paused to flip through the pages of the bid, "looks like two inches of crusher run on the bottom, two inches of three-quarter inch rock over the top, and uh," more paper turning, "then three-quarter inch rolled into the interstices of the larger rock to form a mat which will be compressed to 90 - 100% proctor?"

"Yes, that's right." Ken answered. He submitted the bid fully expecting to sub out most of the work to those in the rock business with equipment. This greatly inflated his bid.

"Our manager from Chicago is going to be in tomorrow and I'd like you and your partner to meet him. How about lunch? You can discuss the details about this parking lot with him."

Lee and Ken met the Chicago manager for lunch.

"You know, Ken, I've got several bids in here that are a lot cheaper than yours." Chicago stated.

Ken didn't skip a beat. "I'm sure you do. But you know what they say, 'You get what you pay for.' I figure if you want the thing to last - it's like anything else . . . you'll spend more money."

"I realize that." Chicago nodded. "After reading your specifications they were far above anything else that was submitted. Most people just said they were going to dump some rock on the lot spread it around about 4 inches thick." The plant reps laughed and everyone continued eating.

Ken performed cool as a cucumber while poor Lee sat across from him sweating bullets. Right about the time everyone finished with lunch, Chicago tossed another monkey wrench into Ken's scheme.

"I'll tell ya what I'd like to do... I'd like to see a couple of the jobs that you guys have done here in town and then we can just go ahead with this."

Lee nearly spit up his coffee. Instead, he excused himself to use the restroom and glared at his partner in crime.

"I have to go, too." Ken added and stood up to follow Lee down the hallway.

"Now what the hell are we going to do?" Lee asked from inside the men's room.

"The only one thing we can do - we gotta lie!"

Ken and Lee hopped into the car with Chicago and the plant reps to drive them around town. A few miles up the road Ken spotted a bank with a brand new asphalt parking lot - and it was beautiful.

"This here is one of our jobs." He pointed to the corner lot. "You can call John Jones over there at the bank and he'll tell you everything you need to know."

"Well that's a beautiful job." The Chicago manager complimented the two men. "I don't think we need to look at anymore. I was pretty convinced you guys could do the job anyway."

Ken and Lee landed their first paving job. The lot design entailed a concrete driveway that led up a hill to a rock parking lot. This required a lot of rock and someone skilled with a grader; Ken called Marve Wallins.

"What would you charge me to grade something like that, Marve?"

"Is that that lot down by that big ol' feed company?"

"Yeah."

"I bid that Goddamn thing! How the hell did you get it?!"

Ken called the rock company and had the same conversation with them. When the job was completed, they had a beautiful, professionally finished lot that they could honestly show off to any potential clients. Ken and Lee made close to $5,000 their first time out. It was fantastic!

* * *

The next bid was for a lot at a large food processing plant. This parking lot included an electric gate. Once again, Ken used the same government jargon and specifications in the bid. Unfortunately, he wasn't sure how to include costs or specifications for the gate.

He decided to do some research. Driving around town he spotted a commercial parking lot with an electric gate and an attendant letting people in and out. Ken parked in the lot and walked over to spark up a conversation with the guy manning the booth for the gate.

"You know, I'll bet these gates cost a lot of money?"

"Yeah, they cost a fortune." The gate controller agreed.

"Any idea how much?"

"I don't know, but I would imagine around $10,000."

That was good enough for Ken. He included the $10,000 figure on his bid. Even after he was awarded the job, he still knew nothing about electric gates.

Before the internet, there was the multi-volume Sweets Catalog: Ken could find nearly anything about construction materials in those books. He located the section on electric gates and the phone number of a Chicago based company.

"Hello! This is Ken with Anderson Paving and Construction. We do a lot of business here in Omaha and we'd like to become a distributor for your gates."

The voice on the other end of the telephone was thrilled with such a prospect. "You would?!"

"Oh yeah," Ken said. "Do you have different models? I don't know too much about these gates."

"The main one that we use –" the voice proceeded to tell Ken about their product line.

"If I were to buy that gate, what does it usually run?"

"Around $3,000."

"Mmhumm. Well, the thing I'd like to do – if it's all right with you – is that I'd like to buy just one gate for a display." Ken explained. "And if you give me a really good break on this first one, then we would be ordering lots of gates from you in the future."

"How about if I send it to you for $1,700?" Ken smiled to himself and the gate company shipped it out the next day.

Ken installed his $1,700 gate and made close to $10,000 in profit on their second job. The new business brought in more money than he made with Farnsworth in an entire year. It made sense to quit his job with Paul and pursue his new venture full time.

Lee was also convinced, so he hung up his tool belt. The two of them proceeded forward with the adventures of Anderson Paving and Construction.

Invention of the '42 Motor Home

1965

One hot afternoon while Ken and Lee thumbed through a Military Surplus catalog, Ken stumbled upon an Army hospital bus for bid at Fort Ord in Monterey, California. Their old '42 school bus had provided countless camping adventures, but it was time to retire it with a newer, larger model. The hospital bus would be perfect.

Ken won the bid and purchased the bus for $400. Now it was time for him and the family to drive to California and pick it up. When they arrived at Fort Ord, the bus actually started right up. After a few minor adjustments, it ran pretty well.

Ken drove the bus while Alice trailed behind in the car. They all followed the beautiful Pacific Coast Highway. After stopping off for scenic views and tourist attractions, they arrived in the Los Angeles area to visit Ken's brother Wayne, before heading home to Omaha.

The Bauer kids found that the overhead baggage racks in the bus made great beds. Meanwhile, Alice and Ken slept on the living room floor in Wayne's house.

During the night a huge windstorm came up, knocking down the concrete wall around Wayne's house and blowing sand into the bus. For years, every time the Santa Ana winds were mentioned, the Bauer's would be reminded of their visit to Uncle Wayne and Aunt Sharon's. The sand that sifted out of all the little nooks and crannies of the bus, as it rambled around the country, wouldn't let them forget.

Like the '42 Chevy school bus, there was a tremendous amount of work that needed to be done before it was fully functional. The bus was a drab olive green both inside and out with large windows and a sunken aisle providing plenty of head room. Once the passenger seats were removed there was plenty of floor space. With a big six-cylinder, low-mileage, 540 cubic inch GM engine mounted in the rear of the bus, it was ideal for a camper conversion.

The door was removed and the entrance space was filled with a hot water heater and a front passenger seat. A new entrance door and stairway was created between the kitchen and living area. Unwanted windows were removed and the holes filled with sheet metal. Sue, Scott, and Sherri all helped after school. Hours of welding and 13 gallons of bondo made a lot of improvements to the exterior.

Ken began painting the bus later that winter in his garage. The 10 foot garage door was high enough to let the bus enter but the bus was way too long for the garage. So he painted the bus in halves: draping visqueen over the entire opening to the garage and taping it to the bus. This kept the warm air contained and after the back end of the bus dried, Ken turned the bus around to paint the other half. He was quite pleased with the end result of his paint job.

Finally it was time for the interior. In the rear of the bus Ken and Alice built bunk beds on each side of the aisle and designed a bathroom. In the center of the bus they installed kitchen cabinets and a stove. Ken found an old Servel gas refrigerator to install in the kitchen. Near the front of the bus they built a u-shaped couch and dining booth (that converted into a large bed) just behind the driver's seat. Ken welded up a 70 gallon freshwater tank that filled the aisle by the couch and a 30 gallon septic tank that went under the bus. Alice fiber glassed both tanks and the shower.

Because there were no RV supply stores at that time for items such as water or septic systems, or doors the Bauer's had to custom build many of the remodeling structures and fittings themselves. It took most all of the money he earned to support his growing family, so all of these additions and refurbishments had to be rationed carefully over a long period of time. The entire family worked on the bus and they completed it over the course of two years.

The big engine in the bus averaged about 5 miles per gallon, up hill or down. The gas tank held about 70 gallons, so they were able to cover around 300 miles between refuels. On their first trip to California the Bauer's drove through Oklahoma, where a gas war was in progress.

"I wonder if you'd consider something for me?" Ken propositioned the owner of a small Oklahoma gas station.

"What's that?" The man looked up at Ken's family staring out of the bus windows.

"Would you give me the truck discount?"

"Nah. That's a volume discount for 50 gallons or more."

"Well, if I can squeeze 50 gallons, will you?"

"Sure. But you ain't gunna use that much gas."

After Ken filled up his 70 gallon tank, paid the man the reduced truck price of .18 cents per gallon, he continued down the highway with his family pulling a Ford van behind them.

Ken had bought the van from the Air Force at Offutt air base in Omaha. The hard top was designed to rise up so the van could be used as a camper. Mostly, it accommodated their family of seven comfortably during trips to the supermarket while leaving the big motor home behind. It pulled nicely behind the bus and didn't affect the gas mileage at all.

Once they arrived in the Los Angeles area and jostled their way through town to Wayne's house, Ken disconnected the van and drove into LA for supplies. Traveling on the freeway the engine quit and Ken quickly found an emergency phone along the shoulder to call Alice at Wayne's house. He asked her to drive the bus over to his location on the freeway, which she did. They backed the bus up to the van, hooked it to the hitch, and continued on their way south.

The kids wanted to visit Sea World so they checked into an RV campground in San Diego. Ken and his eldest son Scott looked over the van's engine and determined it had a broken camshaft. The two of them removed the little six-cylinder engine from the van and placed it on a picnic table in the park to begin disassembling and repairing.

Although the Park owner had a fit when he found out what they were up to, Ken had already purchased a new camshaft and the reassembly process had begun. He and Scott took the engine apart that night and had it reassembled again the next day. They did an excellent job as the little van zipped down the road like new.

Once the kids visited Sea World the next stop on their trip was Mexico! Ken decided it would be wise to purchase liability insurance for the bus before crossing the border. This was an especially good idea because if you were involved in an automobile accident it was not a civil offense, it was a criminal offense – and off to jail you would go until damages were paid.

Ken stopped at a small shanty-looking office building along the highway that had a sign advertising Mexican insurance.

"I only want liability insurance," he told the salesman.

The salesman continued to shove different plans in front of Ken, but they were more than he could afford.

"No, no, I need one for less money." The salesman relented and sold him a plan for $75.

"I know I'm going to regret this," he told Ken. "Every time I sell something this cheap, some crazy driver costs me money."

"Well, don't worry about me." Ken assured him. "I'm a heck of a good driver; I've never had an accident." He lied.

The drive through the guarded gates into Mexico was fairly narrow with a tight 's'-shaped turn. The Mexican guards stood in glass booths near the end of the turn. Ken watched through his right rear mirror to be sure he didn't drive up over the curb.

The left mirror hooked the guard shack and sent it crashing to the ground. An angry guard scrambled out from a shower of broken glass to confront Ken. He looked like a little Mexican jumping bean, although Ken dared not laugh.

The furious guard directed Ken to the detention area where he instructed him to either call his insurance agent or count on spending a lot of time in jail.

Ken found a phone and called the number on the insurance card. While the telephone rang all Ken heard repeating in his head was John's voice… *"Uhh, Missa Kinny…I done had a little trouble on da job."* Although this made Ken smile to himself, he offered a much different explanation to the agent.

"Hello, Mr. Bauer."

"I, uh, got myself into a little bit of trouble over here."

"Already? You left my office, what - 30 minutes ago?!"

"Yeah, I know. But I'm being told that unless you can come to the border guard station with $500, they are going to throw me in jail."

"You've got to be shitting me!" The man hung up with a heavy sigh.

Ken returned the black telephone to its cradle realizing just how humiliated John must have felt all those times. Ken was incredibly grateful when his agent showed up with the $500 in cash after about an hour or so. The Bauer's were allowed to cross the border and spend the next week in Mexico having a great time with all of their kids.

Later, while Ken took in a painted Mexican sunset on a white sandy beach south of Ensenada, he watched the waves break against the shore. This reminded him of another time when his confidence had nearly gotten him into big, big trouble.

Prince Albert & the Rubber Life Raft

1951

Like most young men, sixteen year old Ken and his pals loved firecrackers, skyrockets, or pretty much anything that imploded, exploded or left the ground with excessive speed. It was this love for explosions and his interest in chemistry that encouraged Ken to pursue an adolescent career in the dynamite business.

It was only a few months back when Clarence and Ken tested out their fledgling dynamite crop that had taken them months to engineer and package. They had blown Junior's metal paste bucket ten feet over the Bauer home, scaring nearly half the neighbors to death, not to mention Ken's grandmother. But the boys weren't satisfied with such a trivial demonstration.

Ken pondered this on his way home from school one afternoon. He stopped for a moment at the edge of Junior's driveway, the site of the infamous paste bucket explosion, and considered his options. Standing at the scene stirred his creative juices and he developed an idea.

Ken decided it was time to go fishing.

He went home and made a couple phone calls. Within the hour, Ken, his sweetheart Alice, and Clarence, a one man rubber life raft, and some dynamite, were loaded into Mr. Bauer's Ford.

Just west of town were some lakes the locals referred to as the sandpits. Ken explained that they were headed off to do some fishing; although the poles suspiciously never made it into the Ford.

Ken brought along three full sticks of dynamite, bound them together with masking tape, and placed a detonator in one of the sticks. He explained to his friends that this would probably get some fish. He also brought along a Prince Albert tobacco can filled with their homemade gunpowder that he had equipped with a dynamite fuse.

When they arrived at the lake, Clarence unloaded and inflated the raft. Ken discussed, with enthusiasm, his theory for fishing with explosives.

First, they threw the gunpowder can into the sandpit. It sunk. They waited. Finally, it ignited.

Bllluuubbbbbbb… the gloomy water burped up a few little bubbles as they rose to the surface verifying the unseen explosion. This really disappointed the threesome.

"Did you see any fish?" Ken asked.

"Nope." Clarence answered, still looking out over the lake.

"Well, maybe it just stuns 'em." Ken offered. "Maybe what a guy needs to do - is get out in the life raft, out in the middle of the lake, and we'll throw the bomb out there."

Clarence looked over at Ken with a blank expression on his face. He had a sneaking suspicion that the '*guy*' in the raft, was beginning to look more and more like him.

"…then when the fish come up," Ken continued looking right at Clarence, "you can be right there and you can grab 'em and throw 'em in the boat!"

Ding, ding, ding! We have a winner! He knew there was no sense in arguing once Bauer had a plan in motion.

"Alright . . .sure . . .why not?!" Clarence agreed. "What could possibly go wrong?" He said under his breath. Climbing into the rubber life raft he aimed for the middle of the lake.

Ken and Alice watched from the shore as poor Clarence wrestled with the paddles, struggling because there was no keel on the boat. Clarence paddled on one side, then on the other side and all he could do is paddle himself in circles; he had one hell of a time reaching the center. Once in the middle of the lake he waved back to the couple standing on shore, laughing at his expense.

Alice waved back while Ken reached down to pick up the bomb that rested quietly at his feet. He pulled a book of matches from his front shirt pocket, struck the match, and lit the fuse.

Tossing it out into the lake proved to be much more complicated than he calculated and when he lobbed it out into the water, it ended up much closer to Clarence than he intended. AND his dynamite was made of sawdust, so naturally it didn't sink! There it was - three sticks of dynamite floating there on the surface near Clarence! Ken began shouting to his friend:

"Run, Clarence. Run!"

Alice's mouth dropped open. Helpless, she stared out at Clarence through big, blue silver-dollar sized eye balls.

Clarence paddled like a sun of a bitch until the most enormous explosion interrupted the calmness of the lake. It was as though a depth charge had gone off and all of a sudden there was a wall of water out of nowhere creating a water monster that chased him down! It picked Clarence's life raft up and threw him clear out of his boat. When he surfaced, the only thing the two observers heard from the bank was:

"I'm shot, I'm shot!"

"Swim, Clarence, swim." Ken encouraged his terrified friend. Ken thought he'd killed one of his best friends; he was relieved to see he was alright. And as if that weren't bad enough, the three of them were about to face another problem.

No sooner than Ken and Alice got him safely to shore, the Sheriffs car pulled up. As it turned out, the County Sherriff owned the lake. The waves could still be seen crashing against the shore in all direction from the explosion. The concerned officer politely questioned the kids.

"Have you heard any explosions out here?" The Sherriff asked.

Thinking on his feet, of course Ken was the first to speak out. "Yeah, boy, there was a hell of an explosion over toward the river." Ken pointed. "Maybe if you get over there quick you can catch 'em."

The Sherriff thanked the kids, got back in his car, lights flashing, and headed for the river. Ken, Alice and Clarence watched the officer disappear around the bend.

The three kids hopped in the Ford and raced toward home!

Afterward: *While Ken and Clarence spent much of their early teenage years learning about chemicals and explosives, as adults the two drifted apart. However, when the three were reunited during a high school reunion, they enjoyed reliving many old memories.*

Like much of Ken's adventurous life, Clarence dodged a few bullets of his own. After joining the military and specializing in demolitions, he secured a position at the Pentagon. He later retired, shortly before the 9/11 attacks. Both he and his son (who assumed his father's position at the Pentagon) were both afforded the good fortune of being absent during the historical terrorist attacks.

Joe Mashayda's Hospital Project

1966

Back in Omaha, Ken and Lee had worked together on several projects at the St. Joseph's hospital. It was during that time they came to know and appreciate Mr. Joe Mashayda, the hospital's contracting officer.

Ken knew that having Joe in his corner had a lot to do with the fact he was awarded the job to build a new four-story ER section in the center courtyard of the hospital. The tall, quiet German showed up on the site daily and Ken looked forward to seeing him. Joe would approach in his hospital issued white hard-hat to ask the same question: "What chu making to-day, Ken-ny?"

One of the first projects Joe assigned Anderson Paving and Construction was the development of a water tower base. They were to build the foundation for the hospital's cooling and air-conditioning system.

"Think you can build pyramids – for all deez to sit on?" Joe pointed to the plans. "I get you drawings on where dey need to go."

Ken and Lee hired a foreman by the name of Don Parrott who liked to drink a bit. All three started out forming the pyramid shaped footings. Before they completed the first one, Ken and Lee decided to work on something different.

"Now just continue pouring these footings, Don. We'll be back later." Ken instructed him.

"Okay, sure. I can handle these… no problem." Don waved good bye to Ken and Lee who were headed to the racetrack. Not a good idea.

Joe called Ken the next morning.

"Ken-ny. Were you here when da footings were finished?"

"No, I wasn't, Joe. I let the guys finish them up."

"Mmmhm. Maybe you come down and take a look at this. Tell me what you think?"

Don had formed and poured the pyramids to look like Leaning Towers of Pisa.

"We'll take care of it, Joe." Ken assured him. He called John to come and break them out with a sledgehammer and Don re-poured; this time under closer supervision. With both Don and John on the crew, Ken and Lee decided to stay on site until the water tower base was complete.

* * *

The next project Joe delegated was to extend, and asphalt pave, a section of the hospital parking lot to make it bigger.

"Ken-ny, you think we could make a concrete wall against the dirt bank up there" Joe pointed across the lot, "and pave up to it?"

"Sure." Ken agreed, though at the time he didn't even own an asphalt paving machine. Now it was time that he went to the auction to buy one.

Saturday morning an old Barber Green asphalt finisher came up for sale; he paid $500. This particular piece of equipment sells for $100,000 new, so it wasn't difficult to determine what kind of shape the machine was in, besides the fact that nobody knew how to operate the machine! There were so many levers and pedals – it may as well been from another planet.

Ken had the asphalt finisher delivered to the job site so he and Lee could spend the rest of the weekend trying to figure out how to operate the machine. They drove it up and down the lot with no asphalt in it to get the feel of how to control it.

They rented an asphalt roller. Next, they hired someone with a front end loader to cut the bank back, square up the bank, and prepare for the concrete forms.

"You know, Lee," Ken said surveying the dirt bank, "that wall is only about 4 feet high."

"Yeah?"

"I don't know why we have to form it with concrete forms. I think we can put plywood right up against that bank and pour the concrete between the bank and the plywood." The two green construction owners surveyed the dirt bank and devised a plan.

"Sure, sure." Lee offered. "We could drive some stakes in the ground along the plywood."

"And maybe put some braces out on the end?" Ken added.

"Yeah, that sounds good to me. I think it will work."

Ken delegated a crew to put the plywood in place while Lee ordered the concrete. Once they began to pour the concrete, the plywood – being under enormous pressure - bulged out at the bottom. It even bent the stakes out.

Ken scrambled for the heavy roller to push up against the plywood, hoping to keep it from bulging any further. The Redi-mix truck had to keep pouring, so Ken needed heavy objects to prop in front of the plywood - and he needed them quick! He rushed around the lot, trying to stay ahead of the pour, parking one car after another down the length of the bank.

When the crew stripped the forms the next day, they were as crooked as a dog's hind leg.

"Ken-ny," Joe watched the crew peel back each form, revealing foot after foot of whoop-tee-do's, "you think there's a problem here?"

John busted the wall out and on the second go around both Ken and Lee used industry standard concrete forming techniques to get the job done right.

Joe must have really liked Ken and Lee to consider them for the four-story ER addition. However, before the ER project started Ken found himself in hot water once again.

* * *

The hospital gutters were discolored green and had to be removed before construction could get underway. Ken assumed the hospital had installed galvanized gutters and painted them green.

"I'll take dem old gutters down for you, Missa Kinny an get rid of 'em if you want." John offered. "Even come over tomorrow an I won't charge ya. Maybe eyez sells 'em for a few bucks."

"Alright, John. Sure. Go ahead." Ken agreed, grateful for the time and labor he would save.

John showed up to the job site over the weekend, removed all of the gutters, and hauled them off the scrap yard. He couldn't wait to share the good news with Missa Kinny on Monday.

"Eyez down at da scrap yard on Saturday an I wantsta thank you for dem gutters."

"Oh, sure, John. Why? What did you make on them?"

"Dayz copper gutters." Ken stopped dead in his tracks. John told him how he'd really cut a hat fat hog in the ass on the copper, while Ken kicked himself for not taking a closer look.

John had always sold junk to pick up a little extra money. Once he told Ken about gathering up old, cracked engine blocks to sell for cast-iron over at the junkyard.

"What I does Missa Kenny is I fill dem water jackets full eh sand. Dat makes 'em weigh up real good."

"John, doesn't that bother you to cheat them guys?" Ken asked.

"OH, no – I ain't really cheatin' 'em," John explained, "da more I screwz 'em, da mo money they makes."

* * *

Once the ER construction began, one of the important conditions that Joe specified was there was to be no dirt or dust allowed to get into the hospital.

This certainly created a challenge because the first order of business was to remove two feet of dirt from the site area, which was located in the court yard. The hospital was built around the courtyard and there was no way to get the dirt out, without going through it.

Before the digging started, Ken hung canvas panels down the hallways to prevent dust from entering the building. He also used small power buggies to transport the dirt and tools in and out of the area. Because there wasn't room enough to get an excavator in for the digging, it all had to be done by hand.

The four-story addition was to be built with structural steel beams and concrete decks dividing each floor. Once this was complete the crew built the roof. Although the interior was subbed out to other contractors, this was the first structural steel job Ken and Lee had ever tackled and they were both quite proud of their accomplishments. Additionally, Ken was reminded how deathly afraid he was of heights when he ventured out onto the steel.

Every time he was required to climb along the beams the crew teased him because he looked like a dog with worms! They watched him scoot across a beam, his legs dangling over, while he held on for dear life. It came as no surprise when Ken finally realized that his crew was actually dreaming up problems just to get him out on the beams to embarrass him.

When the project first began, Ken observed his crew and how inept they were at digging out the dirt with their shovels. He thought back to his childhood, watching Donnie's dad, Andrew, digging a grave. There was nobody Ken admired more than Andrew and his crafted technique for digging. Ken decided to give the retiree a call. He convinced Andrew to come join him at the hospital, get on his payroll, and show these guys how to dig a hole.

Andrew showed up with a shovel that sparkled like a surgical tool, all shiny and sharpened, and began his process. Within a couple of days, the old man had finished the hole, and the site was ready for construction.

The Grave Digger

1947

Forest Lawn Cemetery was located six blocks from Ken's home in Omaha, Nebraska. The well groomed location was complete with walking paths throughout the grounds, a Koi pond surrounded by pink and white hydrangea bushes, and thousands of headstones with all kinds of stories buried beneath them. A tall wrought-iron fence stood guard around the entire place and laced its fingers at night when the heavy metal gate closed and locked out all interested parties. Ken and his twelve year old friends discovered adventure both inside and outside of the cemetery grounds.

Donnie's dad, Andrew, was in charge of digging graves for the cemetery. Many times the boys sat on a dirt pile to watch him work. He was a tradesman that took great pride in his craft.

He began by marking out an area of the appropriate size to begin his systematic process. He would use a tile spade to dig out the first layer of soil across the surface. He would then remove the loose layer of earth with a square point shovel. He repeated this process until he had a perfect box-shaped hole of the proper depth. What impressed Ken most was that all of Andrew's tools were like a doctor's instruments; he kept them shiny and sharpened all the time.

One particular visit to the cemetery started with a discussion upstairs in Ken's bedroom. Three boys found themselves bored and uncertain of how to spend their summer afternoon.

"Let's go fish the pond at the cemetery." Gatorbait offered as he lay on his back on the end of Ken's bed, tossing a grass-stained softball in the air and catching it.

Donnie spun around in Ken's desk chair. "I don't want to try that again, no way! The last time we went to that pond, I ended up covered in nettle bumps for a week because of you, Gatorbait."

Ken sat propped up against his headboard with a magazine resting on his knees. "Yeah," he teased Gatorbait imitating him, 'He's after us, he's after us!" he mocked his friend. Donnie joined in on the laughter.

"It's not funny. It coulda been a ghost, you guys." Gatorbait said, now sitting upright and returning the baseball to the floor. The boys had emerged from the tall weeds to come out right near a tombstone. As they did, all three froze when they heard a voice. Most likely a grounds worker, but Gatorbait scared the hell out of his friends when he jumped backwards and took off running.

"You nearly knocked us out trying to get out of there!" Donnie laughed, slapping his knee.

"Even after we passed you up," Ken was laughing between words, "cuz you were trying to get a hold of those britches of yours – and all we heard behind us was 'He's after us, he's after us!' " Ken and Donnie were laughing out loud.

"Awe, you guys were scared too." Gatorbait said looking down at his shoes. "Fine. We won't go fishin' in the pond." He looked up. "How about we fish the creek on the way to see Donnie's dad?"

"Naw, I'm not in the mood for fishin'." Donnie said. "Ken - you got any ammo for your .22? We could do some squirrel hunting down on the creek bank."

"Yeah, I got some. Let me get my rifle," he said, lifting the bedspread to get underneath his bed. "Let's get outta here!" The boys shuffled, single file, from Ken's bedroom.

"There's lots of squirrels in them trees." Gatorbait said on the way down the stairwell. Grandma stopped them on their way through the kitchen, inquiring as to their plans, and insisting on feeding them lunch. After each of them polished off a couple of peanut butter and jelly sandwiches and a cold glass of milk, the squirrel hunters headed to the creek bed on their way to see Andrew.

One thing the boys discovered about squirrel hunting is that they are tricky little devils. As a fella walked around looking for them – the squirrel moved around the other side of the tree watching right back, so you end up circling each other. The trick was to sit down and be real quiet. The boys did just that so they could take turns with Ken's rifle.

"Right there, Donnie" Ken said. Donnie lifted the barrel toward the direction that Ken was pointing. "Pawwwp" he fired the gun and missed the squirrel.

"My turn, my turn" Gatorbait whined.

"Hold on," Donnie cocked the gun, "one more." Donnie pulled the gun from Gatorbait's grip and lined up another target. "Pawwwp." He fired and lowered the gun. "I got him."

"Nope. I think you missed again." Ken said to his friend. "Let Gatorbait try."

Gatorbait dug his rear end deeper into the dirt bank, wrestling and wiggling one butt cheek at a time from side to side to get comfortable.

"What's the matter with you?" Donnie asked, "You got ants in your pants or something?"

Gatorbait paid him no attention. He smiled and rested the gun across his chubby legs and waited for his squirrel.

"Right there!" Ken had spotted another one. "Get a bead on him, Gatorbait."

Gatorbait did as he was instructed, took a deep breath and squeezed the trigger. *Click.*

"Awe, you forgot to load it, dummy." Donnie, having missed both times, said in an aggravated tone.

Embarrassed, but not discouraged, Gatorbait loaded the rifle and waited patiently. He saw his squirrel high up in the leaves of a cottonwood tree. He put his finger back on the trigger and lined his sights on the bushy tailed critter and squeezed. *Pawwwp* went the gun. "I got him!" he said as several leaves fell to the ground, but no squirrel.

"No you didn't. You missed, too." Donnie corrected Gatorbait.

"Let me give it a try." Ken said and claimed his gun from his disappointed friend. There were a couple of squirrels high up in a tree next to the one where Gatorbait had been shooting. He was going to show these boys how it was done.

Ken drew a bead on a large dark colored squirrel, held his breath, and fired. *Pawwwp* - and leaves went everywhere. Tree remnants, along with a dark object, fell toward the ground hitting every branch on the way down.

Hey," Ken said out loud, "I ain't never seen a black squirrel before -" as the animal continued to fall and finally hit the ground with a heavy thud.

"Ah, Jesus Christ, Ken!" Gatorbait jumped up and grabbed a hold of his britches, "you shot someone's tomcat!" and he took off running down the creek bed.

The other two boys followed in a dead run right behind Gatorbait. They reached the edge of the cemetery and stopped at the tall grass where they liked to sneak through the fence. While catching their breath, they all busted out in laughter at Ken's hunting blunder.

"Hey, I got an idea." Donnie said. "Let's not bother my dad today. How about we walk down to the Jewish cemetery and go see my brother."

The other two boys nodded in agreement; they liked Donnie's older brother, Marvin, who was a caretaker at the Jewish cemetery. He told great big tales and scary stories about all the dead folks he tended on the grounds. They were certain that today would be no exception.

They followed the creek bed to the road and walked the half mile to the Jewish cemetery. Once they were on the grounds they spotted Marve right away.

"Hiya Marve!" Donnie shouted, greeting his much older brother.

Marvin was sitting on a granite headstone eating a sandwich. He had a coke bottle sitting next to him on the stone. "What are you scoundrels up to?" he asked the boys.

"We just came to see ya." Donnie said to his brother. "We ain't botherin' ya, are we?" His brother shook his head and took a sip from his coke.

The three thirteen year old boys sat down at Marve's feet and looked up at him eating his lunch. "Does it bother you to sit on someone's headstone like that?" Gatorbait asked the caretaker.

"Nah. They're dead, they don't mind."

"I guess." Gatorbait replied. But Gatorbait's concern sparked a twinkle in Marve's eyes. He was about to head back to work, so he figured he would prime these boys to walk across the grounds with him.

"Well, Gatorbait – you might be on to something." He had the boys' attention.

"What do you mean?" Ken asked his friends wise older brother.

"Some folks might be sensitive to you bothering their stuff." He paused for their expressions. "I can think of one such fella. You ever notice that old stone out there that looks like a big ol' slab laying flat on the ground?"

"Yeah," Ken said, "I know which one you're talking about."

"That's old man Cahn's house." He told the boys.

"His house?" Gatorbait asked.

"Yeah, his house. His grave is his house. Well, he's dead," Marve specified, "but when old man Cahn wants to come out, that slab lifts up."

"Nah uh." Donnie chimed in, looking at his pals to see if they believed his brothers story. They had some pretty big eyes, too.

"Oh Yeah, I've seen it." The caretaker verified. "That slab lifts up and he comes up out of the stairway that goes down in there." Marve crumpled up his paper sack. "It's true fellas." Standing up from his makeshift bench, he grabbed his coke bottle in one hand and stuffed the small ball of brown paper down into the front pocket of his overalls.

"Well, I'd better get to it, boys. You want to walk back toward the tool shed with me?"

The teenagers stood up and brushed off the loose grass clinging to their Levis and began to follow Marve across the grounds. It wasn't a minutes worth of walking before they reached the grave that Marve had described.

"Hey, fellas – that's Old man Cahn's place right over there" he pointed in the direction of a large flat granite slab. Then he grabbed a hold of Ken's shoulder. "Oh my God, Old man Cahn's a commin' out, look at there – I see it lifting up!"

"Holy crap!" Gatorbait squealed, "Let's get the hell out of here!"

They all agreed simultaneously - taking off in the opposite direction from where Old man Cahn was coming up.

None of them heard Marve's laughter echo across the grounds of the cemetery. He watched his little brother and his friends charge off to run six blocks home to safety.

Mudd and the Canadian Stoolspawner

1968

At thirty-four years old, Ken found his appetite for adventure was shared with Omaha friends. One such friend was Howard Tatro, but the guys all called him Tate. He was a lot of things to a lot of people. He was a good friend to Ken, an attentive husband, an involved father, a tropical fish store owner, and most of all - incredibly full of bullshit.

One thing Tate took great pride in was his fish store on Maple Street in Benson, Nebraska. Down the street from his shop was a guy that owned a bar; he was known as Mudd Brueneto.

Mudd happened to be a bit of a local celebrity due to the fact that he was a goalie for the Omaha Knights hockey team. On several occasions he and Tate swapped big fish stories. In the spring of '68, one of their fish tales ultimately turned into a planned fishing trip to Canada.

Mudd gathered up some folks from the bar to go fishing while Tate rounded up Ken and Don. All the fishermen met in the parking lot of the Tropical Fish Store: Mudd in his Cadillac with his fishing crew which included an iconic Omaha TV sportscaster.

Tate and Don boarded Ken's old 1952 GMC school bus. Scott, Ken's fourteen year old son, was already seated at the table waiting to deal a hand of cards to Tate, who'd promised to teach him some poker tricks. Ken finished strapping the 14 foot aluminum boat to the top of the bus.

"Well I guess that's it," Don said closing the door behind him, "nuthin but highway ahead of us boys!"

Mudd and his group rented a cabin on Lake of the Woods, just outside of Kenora, Canada. After several hours of swapping old fish stories and bullshit, the road warriors arrived at the lake. Ken and his crew camped just outside of Mudd's cabin in the bus.

While Mudd's group kicked around in their cabin, the four bus-camping fishermen decided to unload the boat and get a head start on the fishing.

The first to bring in a fish was Tate. He reeled in this funny looking creature that could have been a fish, but it looked more like a cross between an eel and carp. It had a long black body, spiky fins, and an abnormally large, malformed head.

"What in the world is that ugly looking thing?" Scott watched the fish wriggle on the end of the line while Tate reeled it in closer to the boat.

"Awhhh," Tate growled, as the fish flopped down on the bottom of the boat, "that's one of those Goddamned Burbots. They're a stink fish." With one foot on the fish's head, he fought the hook snagged through the side of the creatures gasping mouth. "I don't wanna throw him back. These fish are bad for the lake."

He released the hook from the fish and kicked him aside. Several beers and many gut busting lies later, the fishermen arrived back on the dock. Ken looked down in surprise to see that the Burbott was still alive there in the bottom of the boat; his gills moving back and forth after all that time.

Tate saw him too.

"Whata ya gunna do?" Ken asked Tate, "kill him?"

"No. No, I got another idea."

Tate scooped up the Burbott and headed for Mudd's cabin. The Mudd gang was still out fishing. Ken followed a few curious steps behind Tate, with Don and young Scott close on their heels. Tate carried the barely breathing fish into Mudd's bathroom and plopped him in the toilet.

    "You've got to be kidding?" Ken looked at Don, who shrugged, then took a drink from his beer and walked back to the living room to relax on one of the sofas. Tate and Ken followed suit, grabbing a beer from the refrigerator on their way to claim a spot in front of the television with Don. Three men, one excited teenager, and a fish waited patiently for Mudd and the others to return.

    They didn't have to wait long. Not even two commercials later, the Mudd gang arrived. The large group of men clamored into the cabin disrobing wet clothes and knocking over fishing poles; chattering about starting up a poker game. The drinks were poured, chairs selected, cards dealt, and Mudd decided to use the bathroom.

    From somewhere down the hallway, came the sound Tate had been waiting for.

    "Jee-sus keer-eyest!" Mudd shouted from the bathroom, "would ya look at this!"

    Tate says, "Whatcha got, Mudd?"

    While Mudd zipped up his pants, he craned his neck out into the hallway and answered Tate. "There's something here in the goddamn toilet."

    A curious circle of men exchanged suspicious looks at each other from behind poker hands, cigars, and mixed drinks. Simultaneously, they all jumped up from the poker table to investigate the commode mystery. Tate was in the lead.

Nine flannel-wearing, grungy- bearded heads poked in the bathroom door. Tate says to Mudd, "Oh man, Mudd!" and puts his hand on his friends shoulder, "Do you have any idea what that is?" he asked him.

"No."

"It's a Stoolspawner!" Tate told him.

"A Stoolspawner?"

"Yeah," Tate animates with his hands, "they swim up the septic tank laterals and they get into the stool - and then they spawn!"

"Really?" Mudd doesn't take his eyes off the ugly fish swimming around in the commode.

"Yeah. And this is a female. I'll bet the male is gunna be along any minute." Tate said.

Mudd was buying every word. Why wouldn't he? Tate owns a fish shop, so he's supposed to know all this shit, right?!

"And do you know," Tate maintains, "that nobody has ever got a picture of a Stoolspawner - spawning!" Mudd looks up at Tate. "Not that I know of, anyhow." Tate says.

Several of the other guys had caught on to Tate's joke and wandered back to the living room. Muffled laughter was tightly contained around the poker table.

"Mudd, you take your camera and get a picture." He watched Mudd scurry around like a kid on Christmas morning looking for batteries to run a remote-control toy. "It'll be worth a thousand dollars probably."

With everyone back in the living room, the bathroom was quiet for a few minutes. Mudd remained; camera in hand, pointing it down at a Burbott swimming around in the john.

It didn't take long before Mudd put two and two together. Feeling foolish, he walked the hallway of shame to join everyone back at the poker game. He sat down at the quiet card table; all eyes lowered, smirks thickly traced on every set of lips. Mudd knew he was in for the worst heckling of his life; he'd never live this 'fish' story down.

He picked up his hand, cleared his throat, and calmly shook his head.

"Tate, you son of a bitch."

And with that, the Canadian Stoolspawner heckling began!

The First Amphibian

1968

Ken returned from Canada ready to resume his paving and construction adventures with Lee. Since their business showed signs of steady profit, they began investing in various military surplus equipment purchases. When winter closed down the construction, they spent their time rebuilding and selling equipment.

When Ken arrived at the office, Lee was reading a military surplus catalog lying there on the desk. He had found a large Army boat that was up for sale in Florida.

The boat was called an Amphibian and it was part of an experimental program in the Vietnam War effort. It was designed to work well on land as well as in swamps and other bodies of water. Ken and Lee got excited at the prospect of fishing from such a contraption.

"Hell, Ken, we could just drive it up from anywhere, flip a toggle and be on the water!"

"I'm going to bid $600 on it," Ken informed his partner and within a few days time they were awarded the bid.

In order to get the thing hauled up from Florida, Lee hired a trucking company that had a flatbed semi truck coming to Omaha. They only had one problem: this flatbed had a high 4 foot deck, and although the army base agreed to load the Amphibian, Ken and Lee would have to figure out a way to unload it.

Ken called the Omaha Crane Company and explained his predicament.

"You suppose we could have a piece of military surplus equipment delivered to your yard, have a crane unload it, and then we'll pick it up?" He was granted permission.

Ken explained that the truck would arrive on Sunday but the crane company was closed. Somehow he convinced the manager to come in for an hour and unload the truck.

When Sunday came, the truck was unloaded in the crane company's yard while Ken and Lee stood by to witness the momentous occasion. Their joy subsided once they found out the amphibian would not start. They were going to have to get new parts in order to make the giant toy operable.

Ken made arrangements with the unhappy yard owner to leave the amphibian on the property so that he and Lee could work on it after he was gone. On his way out, the owner handed over a padlock and told them to lock up when they finished.

Fortunately they found the parts needed at a local auto parts store and proceeded to repair the engine. It took much longer than anticipated and they worked well into the night. Once they got the engine running, the temptation to play with their new toy was overwhelming.

"We better figure out how to operate this thing," Lee told Ken. He agreed. So they practiced around the parking lot, jumping and jerking until they had some idea of how to operate it. Time had gotten away from them and it was after midnight.

"I'll betcha I could just drive this thing home," Ken offered.

"I don't see why not," Lee considered. "Doubt there's any traffic out there."

The amphibian was really a strange looking critter. It had sausage shaped rubber tires, on wheels, that were all hooked together so that they would work like a track on a bulldozer. The problem however, was that the track was not flat on the bottom; it was shaped more like the rocker on a rocking chair.

The machine was powered by one GM six-cylinder engine connected to a variable speed transmission. The tracks were operated by two different handle clutches, one for each side of the two tracks. Steering it was similar to a bulldozer where the handle is pulled back to engage whichever track required moving. To go straight ahead, both steering clutch levers are pulled backwards. If you wanted to turn right, the left-hand lever was pulled back, and to turn left, the right hand lever was pulled back.

Ken started driving the Amphibian up Center Street at about 1 o'clock in the morning, still learning how to effectively operate the machine. He figured out that in order to stop he must push the levers forward to apply the brakes. Although that may not sound difficult, it did create a problem.

Center Street dead-ended at 33rd St. at the border of Hanscom Park. Ken approached the intersection just as the stoplight turned red. As he attempted to apply the brakes, he pulled a handle the wrong direction and the thing reared up, like a spooked bronco! It slammed back onto the street with a loud thud, barely missing a police car that had approached on Ken's right side.

Ken got the amphibian stopped and the officer got out of his car.

"Are you crazy?" he appeared somewhat peeved at Ken. "What in the hell do you think you're doing? And what the hell is this damn thing anyway? Do you have a license on it?"

Ken stammered and stuttered but strangely, he was unable to come up with any good answers. Ken stared at the officer, his lips moving as he tried to form words to answer the man. The officer continued to chastise him.

"You can't drive this thing around here. You've got to get this thing off the street right now."

"Yes, sir. Alright." But when Ken tried to move forward with it, he could only turn in circles to the right. As he went around one circle after the other, gaining little ground toward the park with each circle, he finally got the damn thing off the street.

Lee parked his truck and laughed all the way up to greet Ken.

"I hope he doesn't come back, he looked pretty mad at you," Lee said.

"Yeah, we gotta get this thing fixed and get it home." They determined that the drive chain for the right track had broken. Apparently that was a common problem with this vehicle, because spare master links for the chain were included in the toolbox.

After using a nail and rock to drive out the old master link pins, Ken and Lee replaced them and were ready to drive home. Ken looked down at his watch, now it was almost 3 o'clock.

A large crowd had gathered around while they had worked on the machine.

"What in the hell are all these people doing out at 3 o'clock in the morning?" Ken asked Lee.

"What brings you out to the park so late tonight?" Lee asked a young man in Levis and a bright blue T-shirt.

"Are you kidding? You guys are famous, you're on the radio."

"What? What do you mean?" Ken asked the kid.

"The announcer had been listening to a police radio and he said that there was some kind of a nut driving a tank around Hanscom Park."

Ken was surprised at how many people came to see his monstrosity. What concerned him more was the fact that, yes, he may be nuts for driving an amphibian around the park at 3 o'clock in the morning, but what kind of a person got up in the middle of the night to come see a nut in a tank?

Ken fired up the amphibian, drove across the park, and proceeded onto the street that passed in front of his house. He simply parked it in the driveway, said good night to Lee, and went to bed.

The amphibian seemed to be a never-ending source of amazement to the passersby. Lee was also enchanted.

"I suppose we better build a trailer to haul this thing on," Ken suggested.

Lee agreed, "I don't think we want to take her on the road again to get to the lake."

"Nope. Not unless *you* want to take the chance driving it this time."

During their first trip to Carter Lake the two friends had high hopes that the thing would skim along on top of the water. Unfortunately, it hardly moved in the water and when the tracks went round and round, the rubber tires smacked down, shooting water high in the air and soaking its passengers.

They decided to attach Ken's 15 hp Mercury outboard to the amphibian; the idea being that this would push it along in the water. After they hooked the motor up, they took the amphibian out to the Missouri River and launched it.

It turned out that the outboard did a heck of a job of pushing the amphibian in the water, as long as they were headed downstream. But when they turned upstream the damn thing wanted to go backwards with the current. The only alternative was to drive out of the river and up onto land, where the thing could travel.

Now the trouble was there weren't any launching areas or roads. Their only choice was to drive the thing out of the river and up into the swamp that ran alongside the river. Boy did that thing ever work in the swamp!

The tracks went round and round as the tires grabbed into the mud and grass and weeds in the swamp, throwing vegetation 10 feet into the air. Most of the swamp debris landed on top of the amphibian and soon it looked like the creature from the Black Lagoon.

When Ken and Lee finally reached the road they had a visitor waiting for them - the County Sheriff. He had the same questions the officer did down near Hanscom Park.

"What the hell do you guys think you're doing?"

Ken felt like he was six years old all over again.

"You can't drive around through a swamp like this and tear it all up!" After a long lecture on swamp ecology, the sheriff gave them a ticket for harvesting swamp plants.

By and by, Ken ended up in front of a judge. He came prepared to explain to the robed authority figure what they had done and how it happened; he also provided pictures of the creature from the Black Lagoon. The judge laughed so hard, he could hardly hand down his ruling. In between bursts of riotous laughter, he dismissed the case.

    Ken and Lee had several more adventures and they even took the kids out to the lake to enjoy the large swamp creature. But no one enjoyed the Amphibian more than Ken and Lee because it brought out the kid in them as well.

Susie's Story

1969

Ken's eldest daughter, Susan Lynn, came into his life on August 10, 1952. She was a spirited girl who seemed to be following in her fathers' footsteps by obtaining her driver's license on her sixteenth birthday and taking her first solo flight shortly after that.

Ken's flying lessons with Susie finally paid off. He watched his female prodigy take off on her solo flight from the South Omaha airport in a rented Piper J-3 Cub. She ascended up over the trees and disappeared behind them for quite some time. Initially this concerned Ken, thinking maybe she crashed, but when he didn't see any smoke he figured she was all right.

Before long he saw her returning on the horizon and he watched his daughter have a great time flying close to the ground, performing coordinated turns, climbs, and descents, until she circled back around to the corn patch near the landing field. When she came in to land, she was going a little too fast and taxied right into the green cornfield. Ken helped his daughter drag the plane out. With his history, what a special moment the two of them shared with that landing!

Later in the year, Susie attended her high school prom only to return home early. Her house was busy with three little brothers, a little sister and her mom pregnant with another sibling on the way. When she complained of her legs hurting, Ken suggested rubbing some alcohol on them.

"You probably did too much dancing." He teased his teenage daughter.

On the 30th day of January Alice checked into the hospital to deliver their sixth child, Kenneth Harrison. The following afternoon Ken took Susie to the family doctor due to the increased pain in her legs.

The expression on the physicians face will remain with Ken forever. The doctor insisted Ken take his young daughter to the hospital straight away for further blood tests. He never dreamed he would hear such results for one of his children. Ken checked his daughter into the same hospital where his wife and newborn son currently occupied another room.

The procedure was to extract a syringe full of bone marrow out of her sternum. After they were finished, Ken checked in on Susie.

"Dad," she was excited to tell her father what they had done, "you should have been in here! They took it right out of my chest!" Susie wanted to be a nurse, and was already volunteering as a candy striper, so this procedure was incredibly interesting to her.

Father and daughter sat next to each other on the white hospital bed, killing time with laughter. Ken extended his traditional love gesture and reached over to gently squeeze his daughter's knee with a strong hand. Although she tried hard to not let her Dad see how much that gesture hurt her, he noticed.

Finally the doctor came into the room and asked Ken to join him in his office where he lowered the boom. The diagnosis was adult type lymphocytic leukemia. The discussion revolved around medical advancements and how the medical field was on the verge of being able to control the disease and prolong life for a few years. But mainly what to expect and what the cost would be to him and Alice.

Ken had taken his wife and new son home that very morning. Susie's diagnosis had cast a shadow on the joy of a new baby and Ken felt as though he was trading one child in for another. After further conversations with family and professionals, the Bauer's decided to perform more tests, which ultimately yielded the same results.

By the first part of February, the doctor tried a new drug on Susie that he explained would only work once. Susie received two shots at $1,800 apiece and that miraculously gave her a short remission, allowing her to come home.

Ken stayed strong; he tried very hard not to cry around Susie. He also tried to wear an amusingly, hopeful, happy face around his sick child. This was incredibly difficult for him; and although Susie never implied or said anything directly, Ken would later fear he may have given his daughter the impression that he didn't care.

By mid-March Susie was back in the hospital. Several school friends came to visit her, including a boyfriend who sat with her for hours at a time. When Ken's friends would ask what she needed, he was void of suggestions. Tate brought a large stuffed lion and Susie loved it! She named it 'Leo' and Ken was surprised that a sixteen year-old girl would love a stuffed animal. Pretty soon everyone was bringing her stuffed animals until the whole room was with filled with them.

Also, Jeannie Hiukka, a dear friend from Duluth flew in to stay a week; she visited every day and even crawled into bed with Susie to comfort her best friend.

"Do you know what she told me today?" Jeannie asked Ken over a soda in the hospital cafeteria.

"No. What?"

"She said, 'Isn't this something. I haven't even had a chance to have sex yet.'"

Ken spent a lot of time visiting with his daughter as well. One morning during a stroll around the hospital hallways, they recognized the sound of her doctors' voice in front of them.

"…it breaks my heart," Susie's doctor confided in his colleague, "she's only sixteen years old." The two doctors, unaware of who walked behind them, spoke back and forth about the fatal granulocytic Leukemia (CML) and Susie's tragic case, while never mentioning her name.

"They were talking about me, weren't they, Dad?" Ken helped his daughter back into bed. "Does that mean I'm not going to live as long?"

Ken's heart broke into a thousand helpless little pieces. "No. It doesn't mean that." He sat down in a chair to face his daughter. "It just means they're going to do something different."

"Like what?"

"Probably use some different drugs." He suggested. "They're just discussing how to handle it differently, sweetheart."

"I don't know. He seemed pretty sad."

As expected, Susie's condition worsened. Near the end of March, the Bauer family packed for a trip to the City of Hope medical center that was testing a new drug that might help Susie. Alice boarded a flight with baby Kenny and Susie while Ken drove to California with the rest of the children.

Other than a terrible bout of airsickness that Susie suffered during her flight, she appeared to be feeling much better after arriving at the cancer clinic. To be near Susie the hospital arranged for everyone to stay in a little cottage at the City of Hope.

Some of the drugs seemed to be working for her. But Ken continued to search the world over for leukemia cures. He discovered a doctor in Japan who had a sister that had been diagnosed with the disease. The siblings both had the same blood type, so the doctor did a reverse transfusion where his blood was transferred into his sister, while her blood was transferred back into him.

The theory was that his immune system worked properly and it would fight the agents in her blood and then after six weeks they performed another reverse transfusion. She had immediate remission. This experimental procedure took place a year before Susie's diagnosis and the Japanese sister was still in remission.

Ken and his daughter both had A-positive blood. It didn't take Ken long to confront the doctor about trying the reverse transfusion with him and Susie.

"It's against the law, Ken. We cannot risk the life of one patient to save the life of another."

Ken relentlessly pleaded with the doctor until he at least agreed to study the case. The doctor discovered that the same tests had been conducted at the University of Chicago with three different sets of test subjects. The first set of subjects experienced remission while the other two sets came down with leukemia.

Ken persisted, willing to do anything to save his daughter. "It would give her a chance to live. She's sixteen!"

"I'll tell you what I will do," the doctor compromised, "I'll talk this over with Susie. She'll be informed of all points, good and bad. Then we'll let her make the decision."

Susie was adamantly against the idea; unwilling to risk her Dad's life to save her own. Ken begged the doctors to use their new experimental drug on her.

"This drug is only going to make her incredibly sick. And the reality is," the doctor paused, "she has to be alive for six weeks for it to even take hold. I can't keep her alive that long."

The doctor reached out and placed a hand on Ken's shoulder.

"Ken. Susie is dying." The unimaginable words surged through Ken's veins like ice water. "The best thing that we can do for her is to keep her comfortable and keep the pain down. Pretty soon she'll become resistant to the morphine. The longer she lives the harder it's going to be on her."

The family had several good days sitting around, talking, laughing, and enjoying each other's company in the little hospital room. On several occasions Susie's siblings mentioned Disneyland.

"Mom, Dad," Susie selflessly encouraged her parents, "you should take them and go have a good time."

Ken wanted to be with Susie. However, the three of them finally agreed that the kids should go see Disneyland while Alice and the baby stayed behind for an afternoon. Nobody anticipated that Susie was so close to death. While Ken toured the four older kids around Disneyland, Susie died in Alice's arms.

Guilt comes naturally for any parent who loses a child. Even after years had passed and still, there was no cure,

Ken blamed himself for not looking harder to save his daughter.

    To outlive a child is a most unnatural experience. On April 3, 1970 Ken discovered this when he lost his beautiful, spirited angel to leukemia.

Part Four

The Asphalt Business

Fire Up the Distributor Truck

1970

For quite some time after his daughter's death, Ken attempted to deal with his grief by using distraction techniques and transporting himself to happier places in his mind. This sometimes left him feeling guilty as well, so he decided to throw himself into his work.

Evolving from the construction business into the asphalt / paving business progressed quite naturally for Ken. Of course that didn't alleviate of any his fancy foot work while dodging various problems along the way.

Ken bid an asphalt overlay job for a grocery store parking lot on 72nd street, but the job was too big for him and his crew to handle. He needed more equipment so he purchased a 1939 Chevy distributor truck from the auction. It was a real piece of junk.

The vehicle was covered bumper-to-bumper with thick black asphalt. It also came equipped with a thousand gallon, tar- encrusted tank mounted on the back, and it had no front window. When the distributor truck showed up on the job site Monday morning, it fit in nicely with the rest of the motley crew waiting to work.

In order to get started, the existing asphalt surface had to be coated so that the overlaid asphalt would adhere to it. This required a process called tack coating, a method that has changed tremendously over the years.

Ken chose a fast dry product that reduced the tracking when cars drove over it, but there was a downside. Once it was shot onto the ground the evaporating Naptha was incredibly flammable.

With everyone on the job site prepared to start tack coating, Ken instructed John to drive the distributor truck while Al operated the tank on the back. On older models, the spray bar, with a 4 foot lever, was located on the back of the truck. Directly behind the valve was a platform where the operator could stand.

John fired up the distributor truck; meanwhile, Al hung onto the back. With the exception of the white colored scars on his dark face, which he had acquired in his younger years of razor fighting, Al's skin was barely discernible from the tar on the truck.

Once the truck was in motion, Al gripped the lever and opened the valve. The two men made several passes close to the building. The grocery store was open for business while they were working on the lot. A customer happened to walk out of the store just after John made a fresh pass in front of the sidewalk. The man flipped a cigarette butt onto the wet parking lot.

WhhhhhooooFFFFFFF!

The pavement started burning. John and the noisy distributor truck rolled forward continuing to spray, unaware of the flame. The fire chased after them threatening to catch up. All Ken could do was jump up and down and holler at Al to close the valve.

Somehow, Al turned in time to see the flame charging toward him. He managed to shut off the asphalt flow as John continued to drive forward unaware of what had happened.

Ken threw his head back in relief. He had a feeling this would not be the last of the asphalt screw-up's in his future.

Hinky Dinky & the White Convertible

1973

Turns out the asphalt funnies continued over the years and one of the most memorable events happened to John during another grocery store parking lot job.

The Hinky Dinky grocery store, located at 72nd and Dodge St. in Omaha, needed their parking lot patched. This required a different technique than paving a lot.

First, all of the loose asphalt must be removed from the chuckholes and then the edges must be tack coated. Ken would have John dunk a broom into a bucket of tack coat and smear it around the edges, preparing the holes for the new asphalt patch to stick properly.

Operating under the assumption that a task involving a bucket and a broom would keep John out of trouble for an afternoon, Ken left John in the Hinky Dinky parking lot to begin patching holes. An hour later, quietly camouflaged under paperwork deep within his office, Ken received a phone call.

"Missa Kinny, we done had little trouble on da job."

"Jesus Christ, how could you get into trouble over there? You weren't even driving anything!"

"It wuddn't my fault, Missa Kinny. Honesta God. I was out there wid da bucket - an I was tackin' 'round dat hole out there an I was jus about finished, an I look over my shoulder an here comes dis woman in dis white convertible . . ."

Ken let out a long heavy sigh and leaned back in his chair to hear the rest of the tale. "Mmm hmm."

"Missa Kinny, I hada jump out da way! She hit dat bucket an da bucket done flipped up in da air an landed upside down right in da front seat wid her! She had dat tar all ova her white sweater an dat pretty white leather apolstry"

"Ughhhh. Ken groaned. "Well who is she?" He asked John.

"Dammed if I know. An I wadn't gunna stick 'round to find out - sheez mad as an ol' wet hen!"

Swift Packing Company

1971

    Regardless of John's antics, everyone seemed to love the big guy. He was notorious for making questionable judgment calls, other times he was downright bewildering, and quite often he was terribly expensive when it came to maintaining equipment.

    Ken owned an old vintage International single axle dump truck. The maximum load capacity was around 8 tons but Ken encouraged his drivers to carry 12 tons. This was of course to get more asphalt onto the job in fewer trips, equating to a cheaper transportation bill.

    On a rather large job in downtown South Omaha, Ken prepared to leave the job and return home for the day.

    "Why don't you take the truck to the asphalt plant, John and get another load of asphalt." Heading toward his car, he added over his shoulder, "Make that the last one for the day."

    "Okay, Missa Kinny."

    Ken pulled into his driveway and got out of his car. On the way to the front door he brushed the dog hair from his pants. He had been petting his German shepherd, Tomahawk, back at the plant. He barely made it through the door before the phone rang.

    "Missa Kinny, I done had little trouble on the job." John called Ken from a telephone booth located across the street from the Swift packing company.

    "Jesus Christ, John! What'd you do?"

"It wuddn't my fault, Missa Kinny. . ." Ken listened to John pant while he told his story.

"You know I was comin' down that 28th street an I had dat 12 tona asphalt on dat truck . . .

"an you knows you wudn't sposeta have no 12 ton on dat truck – 8 tons all we spose to haul! …you always make me haul 12 ton –"

"Jesus Christ, John – what happened?"

"Well, eyez drivin' down that 28th street an it started rainin' an there's those bricks, an dat rain makes those bricks in dat street real slickery. . .

"well, I came to dat Swift packn company right there on da end a 28th where it meets da Q Street -"

"Yeah?"

"I put on da brakes but dat damn truck didn't stop for da Q Street."

Ken closed his eyes and listened into the phone.

"I bump right into dat wall of dat ol' meat-packin' company."

"Holy mackerel, John. Are you all right? Did the truck hit the building?"

"I'm okay. It didn't hurt dat much. But I can seez the truck's buried in bricks."

"What?"

"Yeah, I think da front end of da truck is in the sausage room!"

2,000 lb Rubber Ducks

1973

Buying from the military surplus was a lot of fun for Ken and Lee, especially when they scored real bargains. However, finding the bargains got to be tricky because the government buried them in bid invitations. Normally the items of interest were airplanes and construction equipment, but nearly anything imaginable was available in those catalogs. So if it were something fun to buy it didn't take much to convince Ken to bid on it.

One day they were visiting in their office and Lee happened upon some military surplus decoys up for bid.

"Decoys?" Ken looked up from the prints spread out on his desk.

"Yeah. We don't have any decoys. Maybe we oughta get some." Lee swiveled around in the office chair, extending the bid to Ken.

Ken grabbed the bid and looked it over. "Boy, there sure must be a lot of them. Says here there's 2,000 lbs in a box and the boxes are 6' x 6' x 6' and they're selling six boxes."

"What do you think they'll take for 'em?"

Ken visualized a crate of duck decoys in his mind and began calculating. "Why don't we bid $25 apiece for them?"

"Alright," Lee said, snatching the bid back and filling it out.

Sure enough, the government awarded the bid to Lee and Ken and later they discovered that each crate cost the government $10,000 apiece.

They sent John with a semi to pick up the crates from Fort Leonard Wood, Missouri. He returned with the cargo and made his way directly into the office to debrief Missa Lee and Missa Kinny. After accounting for every mile of the trip, something didn't add up for John.

"Dems real heavy." John reported. "You says deyz ducks?

"They're decoys, John." Ken answered. Secretly, Ken had been curious to peek inside the crates from the moment the bid was awarded and now they were here. "Let's go out in the yard and open one up and see what the hell they look like."

John followed Ken and Lee out into the yard where the wooden crates awaited. John took a crowbar and pried off the top of one. All three looked down into the crate and inside was thick green rubber folded over on top of itself.

"What the hell is that?" Lee said. He started lifting layers of the heavy green material and exposed a rubber hose measuring about an inch in diameter. It was doubled over and tied with heavy string.

"Maybe you inflate them." Ken offered. "Go around there and get the pavement breaking compressor, John."

John returned with the compressor and Ken proceeded to blow up the green rubber now hanging over the edges of the crate. As air circulated around inside the rubber, the thing started growing out of its crate. The weight of it finally broke the crate down flat.

John and Lee carefully pulled the crate away so the nails wouldn't puncture the rubber. When that first arm of rubber came out and fully inflated, another hose, with another string, came out behind it. Ken stuck the compressor nozzle into the second hose and blew up that piece, and then another piece came out, and another and another. Until eventually a long cylinder that looked like an artillery barrel popped out.

"That don't look like no duck I eva saw!" John was still expecting a decoy, while at this point it was obvious to Ken and Lee they purchased some kind of military cannon replica. Lee continued inflating the barrel and the damned thing extended out 60 feet! This thing was huge! Eventually they had inflated a rubber mockup of a 157 mm track mounted artillery piece.

The comical part was after the rubber monster was complete. The three men stood staring at a gigantic artillery piece with a 60 foot long barrel that refused to stand out straight. The government sold them an impotent cannon!

The last pieces of rubber lying on the ground looked like big green balloons. As John inflated them they formed into artillery shells.

"What are we going to do with all these things?" Ken asked Lee.

"Maybe we can sell them to someone."

"For what?"

"Maybe we can sell them over at the shopping center for a giant Cannon Towel sale!"

"Here's another thought." Ken said, slightly amused. "Why don't we get some pictures so we can show it around."

On his way back to the office to look for the camera, Lee passed Alice heading for Ken with a brown bag lunch in hand.

"Hey, Alice!"

"Hi, Lee. What in the devil are you two up to now?"

"Taking pictures of our cannon. You like it?"

Lee returned with a camera in one hand and a cane fishing pole in the other. Ken ate away at his tuna on white while Alice took Polaroid's of the mounted artillery piece.

Lee positioned himself at the far end of the barrel with the fishing pole; lying down on the ground, he hooked the end of the barrel to the end of the line and held it up in the air so the barrel would be straight. While Ken and John laughed at Lee's antics, Alice managed to get some decent pictures.

"You know, I think I know who would buy that." Alice said looking over the Polaroid's.

"Who?" Ken asked through a mouthful of potato chips.

"I'll bet you could sell it to the movie studios out in Hollywood. They might want something like that for a military movie." Alice mailed off letters and pictures to several movie studios. Weeks later a man working at Universal Studios contacted Ken.

"I see you've got some rubber cannons." He said. "You know we've got rubber tanks and we've got rubber jeeps but we haven't got narry a single rubber cannon."

Ken sold every crate at $600 apiece and Universal Studios even paid extra to have them delivered. What really sweetened the deal was Ken had purchased a piece of equipment on another California base that needed to come back to the lot. This way he got paid coming and going!

He delivered the cannons to a studio set on the California/ Arizona border. The film called for a setting with large sand dunes and they opted for the Buttercup Valley area. This location featured Ken and Lee's rubber cannons along with several other rubber military accessories in a WW2 movie called *Tobruk*.

When Ken returned to Nebraska, Lee caught him by surprise.

"We should buy some more of those rubber cannons."

"Are you crazy, Lee?! We were damn lucky to get rid of those."

Lee wasn't convinced. Seduced by an attractive profit margin, he wanted to get his hands on some more. "Well, I'm going to buy me some." And that is exactly what he did, only he purchased replicas of Sherman battle tanks; with the first of several arriving mid June. As luck would have it, a guy setting up a fireworks stand down on 13th street sparked an idea.

Lee drove down and talked with the owner of the little rickety stand and convinced him to mount one of his rubber tanks up on the roof. What a site! The tank ended up being bigger than the fireworks stand. It looked like it was crushing it like a bug – but boy, did that draw the attention! It was the best thing the fireworks peddler could have ever bought.

Lee was unsuccessful in selling the rest of his stock pile over the next several years.

By now Ken was flying helicopter tours over the Grand Canyon where he had been picked up by a film crew to assist with some stunt filming.

Mega Force was being shot in the Nevada desert. The studio recruited Ken to fly with some extra cameras. The idea was to have flying motorcycles swoop down and attack the rubber tanks on the ground with rockets and different explosives. They needed several angle shots from the air.

The studio asked Ken if they could paint water-soluble camouflage on his brand new A-Star helicopter. However, on the day of the shoot, the director broke his leg and they couldn't use the helicopter. The filming was put off, so the camouflage painted helicopter would have to wait for its glory.

"Go ahead and leave that camouflage paint on there." The artist instructed Ken. "It's a tremendous amount of work, so if you could just keep it on there, I'd really appreciate it . . . shouldn't be more than a couple days before we start rolling again."

Ken agreed. Unfortunately, his helicopter had a turbine engine that smoked like hell and it didn't take long to completely cover the backend of the tail boom with black soot. His helicopters were normally cleaned as part of the daily inspection, but Ken made an exception given the circumstances.

The crew called and informed him they were scheduled to resume filming in a few days. Meanwhile, he was flying tours over the Grand Canyon and got caught in a thunderstorm. That certainly screwed up their nice paint job! All that paint ran down the sides of the helicopter turning it green and black. Ken took it back to his hanger and had his mechanic wash it off.

While Ken stood by listening to the camouflage artists piss and moan about repainting the helicopter he overheard someone discussing their shortage of tank decoys. He knew someone who could help them out.

Ken placed a call to Lee and connected him to the prop director and they made a deal. Lee sold every last tank he had stored in his yard. Everybody was happy . . . until the crew began filling the decoys with air.

Lee stored the crates at his forklift repair yard. Apparently there had been a bit of a mouse problem. The special effects crew ran around bitching about little holes keeping them from inflating their props. They were really pissed off.

"Why don't you just patch it up with some green canvas?" Lee suggested when he got the angry phone call. "I actually have some if you need it. Just glue a patch on there and camouflage over the patch." The repair worked beautifully. Even more impressive than the patch job was the explosives the special effects crew came up with.

They filled the tanks with a mixture of air and flour. Then as the film rolled, the director would send a flying motorcycle to dive down toward a tank. These motorcycles had rockets and appeared to fire their rockets while one of the special effects crew would shoot the tank with a tracer bullet. This bullet ignited the air/flour mixture causing a fiery explosion. As the tank exploded the helicopter mounted-camera passed close, expecting to capture an extraordinary shot.

What started out for Ken as a bargain on military decoys in Nebraska, ended up as one hell of a thrill out in the Nevada desert. Ken was always lucky in that respect. Even during his childhood he would start out on one adventure with his friends and before he knew it, they wound up on an entirely different course.

Taking the Long Shot

1948

This was a sad time for Ken's mother and her thirteen year old son. It was the year that the Bauer's moved Grandpa Smith in with them because Grandma Smith died. Before they could make this transition, much of Grandpa's belongings had to be sorted in preparation to sell his house.

Ken enjoyed the sorting part. He sat with his grandfather, sifting through dozens of boxes and old trunks filled with mysterious treasures, while he listened to the old man tell his tales of times past.

There were many interesting things in Grandpa's treasure trunks. To this day, hanging on Ken's wall is a copy of the Ulster County NY Gazette dated January 04, 1800. It highlights such accounts as George Washington's funeral, slave auctions, and ads for interesting products ranging from corsets to woodstoves.

Ken also discovered things like old match books, pocket knives, and some old .22 shells with no bullets in the end. He stuffed several things in his pockets that would end up in a Prince Albert tobacco can, living under his bed for many years. Naturally, it was the .22 shells that peaked Ken's interest.

Rather than having bullets in them, they had a piece of paper crimped in the ends. Gathering a handful of the shells, he figured these were blanks and later on he could have some fun with the guys. What Ken did not realize, was that these were long rifle size rather than the shorts that were normally used for blanks.

With those blank .22's in his pocket, Ken thought of his neighbor Junior, who was known for being a real prankster. Ken remembered back to an afternoon he spent with Junior watching a western on television that featured a bank robbery. He recalled Junior's attention being interrupted.

Craning his neck to look out the window, Junior noticed a woman at the end of his drive coming toward the house to deliver telephone books. He leaned over and grabbed his .22 that was propped up against the sofa.

"Hey Kenny, watch this!" Junior said with his rifle in hand. He reached over and turned the volume way up on the TV. The bad guys were closing in on the good guys and everyone was hollering. Junior hollers real loud toward the door as the woman stepped up on the porch, "Move out of the way and I'll get 'em!" Then he put the rifle to his shoulder, aimed at the TV, and shot the gun.

Blammm!! The sound of the gun exploded. That gal dropped her phone books on the porch and ran off screaming down Junior's driveway!

Of course they were only blanks, but that poor lady didn't know that, nor did Ken at first. Once he realized what Junior had done, it was the funniest thing he'd ever seen.

Standing there next to Grandpa Smith, with his handful of blank .22 shells, Ken smiled thinking about that afternoon with his crazy neighbor. He squeezed the casings tight in his palm, his excitement growing as he thought about his plans to go camping the next day. He was going to pull that same prank on some of his friends!

Late the next day, Donnie and Ken met Gatorbait at his house.

"Hello Mrs. Gaythe." Ken greeted Gatorbait's grandmother at the front door. Grandma Gaythe had raised Gatorbait and she had always been hard of hearing. She carried around a small square box with a lanyard that hung from her neck with wires that trailed up into both of her ears.

Grandma smiled at the two boys and opened the screen door. Her grandson, Jack, was kneeling down to roll up his pack for their outing.

Gatorbait tied off his pack and stood up to face his smiling grandmother. He mouthed something to her while she scrunched her eyes and leaned in slightly toward her grandson. She couldn't hear him.

So Gatorbait mouthed something else and animated with his hands. Mrs. Gaythe reached for her hearing box to turn up the volume. Gatorbait mouthed another sentence and she shook her head and turned the device up again.

Ken and Donnie stood on the porch, looking away from the old lady, pressing their lips tight to conceal their giggling. Once Grandma had her device turned up full blast, Gatorbait shouted:

"I SAID GOODBYE, GRAMMA!"

"Oh, Jack!" she jumped. "You got me again." Embarrassed, she reached for her aid to turn it back down. The boys waved on their way out the door and proceeded down the street to the Bauer home.

Three excited teens spread their camping gear all over the front lawn to organize for their trip. Mr. Bauer had picked up a pup tent and a couple of soldier army survival kits at the military surplus store for the boys. The kits contained canteens, little cooking pots, bed rolls, and such.

Donnie carried the tent and the other boys divided up the rest. Ken also rounded up his .22 rifle for the adventure.

"We'll shoot us some turtle doves for supper," Ken said.

His father laughed under his breath knowing how many doves it would take to feed those three boys. Besides, the missus had insisted on a couple of apples and some ham sandwiches to take along so they wouldn't starve tonight. Mr. Bauer said nothing and instead wished them a good trip.

They were headed for the railroad tracks. The boys scouted a good camp spot a few weeks back, located near a creek, and less than a mile hike from home. It would be dark in a couple hours so they all agreed it would be best to get going so they could set up camp, hunt some doves and get them into a boiling pot. With so much to get done tonight, Ken decided that the blanks would have to wait until tomorrow.

Having shot 6 little doves on the way to camp, they knew the first item of business was to get a fire going and a pot of water boiling. After seeing the amount of meat in their camp pot, the boys were certainly thankful for Mrs. Bauer's sandwich. But the plan was that they would eat their kill - and use the sandwich only as a last resort.

"*Euwwww!*" Gatorbait was the first to try the boiled dove. "This is awful." He said with a turned up face.

The other two tried a bite of the dove which produced the same reaction. With no seasoning, it may as well have been boiled owl. So the boys gratefully ate their sandwiches, stoked up their fire, and laughed into the night until they fell asleep under a large blanket of Nebraska stars.

The next morning the late sleeping campers gathered up their stuff once the sun had become too warm to ignore. They decided to follow the tracks back home while enjoying their apples for brunch.

As usual, Gatorbait was lagging behind, pulling up his pants and gawking around. Ken had a thought. He pulled Donnie aside to share his secret about the ammo.

"You know what would be really fun?" Ken asked Donnie once he told him about the blanks in his pocket. "Let's you and I pretend to get in a fight."

"Ok, then what?"

"Well," Ken continued, "then I'll take off down the tracks and you shoot me with one of those blanks." He handed the gun to Donnie. While Donnie loaded the gun, Ken continued. "I'll drop down like I'm killed and we'll scare ol' Gatorbait to death!"

So they walked on a bit longer to get further ahead of Gatorbait. Once Ken started the fake argument, Donnie and he went back and forth for a minute. Then, as they agreed, Ken took off running down the tracks.

"Hey, what's going on?" Gatorbait hollered. Then he saw Donnie lift the rifle and aim it at Ken! "Donnie!" he yelled as the gun went off.

Kablamm!

Donnie lowered the gun and giggled quietly. He looked back to see that Gatorbait had eyes as big as silver dollars.

"*AWwwhhhhhh!* You son of a bitch – you shot me!" Ken screamed and rolled around on the ground.

Man, he's really good at acting, Donnie thought. Any minute now Ken would laugh at Gatorbait – but that wasn't happening. They had another problem.

Although they had accomplished scaring the bejeezus out of Gatorbait, the problem was that the shells with paper ends (that Ken thought were blank) were actually full of birdshot! So now Ken had a back full of birdshot and there was no way Ken could go home and tell his parents. They would take his gun away for sure. So the boys had to come up with a plan.

They walked back to Ken's house and ever so quietly headed upstairs to his bedroom. They made it past Grandma who was humming as she cooked away in the kitchen. The three of them looked around for surgical tools to get the birdshot out of Ken's backside. There in his bedroom Gatorbait found a drafting compass with a sharp point on one end.

"Here is a razor blade." Donnie said. He had found Ken's model airplane building kit. He added the blade to the surgical collection on Ken's night stand. Now all they needed was an antiseptic.

"I don't think I have anything up here that will work." Ken told his friends.

Then Gatorbait held up a bottle. "Will this work?" The three exchanged looks over the bottle of formaldehyde in Gatorbait's hand.

"I guess it will have to do." Donnie said. "Give it to me. Now go get a clean T-shirt out of Ken's closet." He instructed Gatorbait. Then he turned to Ken. "Lie down on your bed and try to be quiet."

Donnie took the clean shirt from Gatorbait and wiped all of the tools down with formaldehyde. Meanwhile Ken buried his face in his pillow and prepared for the worst. Nurse Gatorbait stood by to gather the birdshot into his hand.

Fortunately, Ken had been wearing a belt, so most of the birdshot was buried in the leather – but the areas above and below his belt had about a half a dozen bb's for Donnie to dig out.

"Hold on, Ken" he told his friend as he prepared to pour some formaldehyde on his back, "this might hurt."

Wow! The formaldehyde really burnt Ken as he howled into his pillow. Then there was the operating. Donnie would dig down with the drafting compass and pull up a piece of birdshot still attached to skin, and then he would cut it off with the razor blade and hand it over to Gatorbait.

Muffled screams filled Ken's room.

Pretty soon Grandma was hollering up the stairs, "Ahhhwk! What jou kids doin' up there?"

"Nothing Grandma. Ken said, lifting his head from his tear stained pillow trying to steady his voice.

"Jou get down here for lunch."

"Ok, Grandma." Ken answered. Then he told Donnie to hurry up before they get caught.

"I'm almost done. This is going to scar, you know - won't be able to hide that."

Gatorbait giggled.

"What?" Ken turned to his chubby little friend, "what is so funny?"

"I was just thinking." Gatorbait giggled again, looking at the bloody birdshot in his hand. "You'll have the scars to prove now that you are an official pain in the ass!"

Drunken Davenport Mechanic

1973

Not long after purchasing the rubber cannons, Ken bid on four 6 x 6 deuce and a half military vehicles: known to civilians as a two and a half ton truck. The government awarded him all four vehicles and because they were located at an arsenal in Davenport, Iowa – another road trip was in order.

Donnie Wilson offered to go and drive one of the trucks back. Ken recruited a couple of his employee's and his mechanic who had a bit of a drinking problem.

Ken pulled the mechanic aside the night before the Iowa trip and made him promise that he would be stone cold sober the next morning to go get the trucks. The mechanic agreed.

The five men drove to Davenport in Ken's car: Donnie, Ken, two other employees, and the mechanic. Their trip went surprisingly well. They arrived safely on the lot, all four trucks fired right up, and the fuel tanks were topped off for the journey back home.

It was late in the day when they merged onto the I-80 freeway. The mechanic was in the lead truck, Ken and Donnie right behind him in trucks two and three, and the fourth truck bringing up the rear. Ken's car followed the entire convoy.

A few hours into the evening, right around dusk, Ken's mechanic began to drift across the lanes in front of him until he was crossing over into the median.

From in the median, the truck eased over into the other lane, right into oncoming traffic! He then drifted back on to the median and then right back into the oncoming traffic again! Ken watched in horror. Within a few seconds the truck drifted back onto the median to cross back in front of Ken and Donnie.

Both Ken and Donnie had slowed to watch the truck in front of them. They pulled up next to one another and rolled down their windows.

"Dammit, Kenny – he's going to hit somebody!" Donnie shouted.

"Yeah, I don't know what's the matter with him."

"We need to catch up with him so I can try to jump in there and get that truck stopped." Donnie hollered.

Ken nodded and motioned for Donnie to pull over. Donnie shut down his truck and jumped into Ken's. The two men continued down the stretch of highway, fearful of what waited ahead of them.

They spotted the meandering truck at the bottom of the next hill. As luck would have it, it had slowed down; still traveling in the middle of the median where the soil was soft and muddy.

Ken pulled alongside of the truck and distressed driver. Donnie opened the passenger door and like Indiana Jones, he jumped onto the running board of the truck, opened the driver side door, pushed the incoherent mechanic out of the way, and climbed in to stop the truck.

While Donnie wrestled with the hand throttle that had been acting like a cruise control, he hollered at the driver. The mechanic was unconscious, so Donnie led the convoy to the nearest hospital.

It turned out the drunken mechanic was used to having such a large volume of alcohol absorbed into his system that his blood sugar dropped dramatically from not drinking. This resulted in a state of unconsciousness, which the doctor rectified with an IV drip of some kind of glucose, and then turned him loose.

Who would have ever thought a promise not to drink could end up nearly getting someone killed?

Tarred & Feathered

1973

There were few dull moments in Ken's asphalt business. A particularly fond memory was an armor coat job where the streets inside of a trailer court needed paved; referred to nowadays as chip sealing.

Ken used his distributor truck to shoot SC (Slow Cure) cutback asphalt onto the existing gravel or rock and then put a layer of sand and gravel over the top of that. However, for this job his distributor truck was on the fritz, not to mention how embarrassing it was to have that dirty ol' windowless truck on the job. Ken took a chance and called his friend, Marve Wallins.

"Is there any chance I can borrow that old distributor truck you've got, Marve?"

When it came to the importance of cleanliness in equipment, Marve and Ken were on opposite ends of the spectrum. If Marve drove the distributor truck himself he would never get a drop of asphalt on anything: not on himself, not on the equipment, nowhere but the intended asphalt destination. Ken admired this about Marve and he wondered how in the world he accomplished such meticulousness. The bottom line was that Marve was incredibly particular about not having asphalt, anywhere, in his truck.

"I'm not going to let you take my truck out and get it all messed up with asphalt." Marve teased Ken.

"Oh no, Marve - I won't do that. You know me better than that!" Ken laughed. "I promise, I'll take good care of it."

"Okay. I'll lend it to you." Marve offered, and then added: "but when you come back pull up in the yard. I'm going to dump 50 gallons of diesel fuel in there and I want you to jog it around -back and forth out on this washboard road coming into my place. Then squirt it back out on the road and that should clean the truck out."

Ken finished up with Marve's distributor truck and he and John drove back to Marve's lot. On the drive over, Ken felt quite proud returning the truck with not a drop of tar anywhere.

They used most of the asphalt out of the tank except for little bit lying in the bottom and Ken wanted to get that cleaned out. He directed John to retrieve the 50 gallons of diesel fuel Marve requested of him and the two drove the truck around on the washboard road.

"John? Do you know how to fold up those bars?" Marve's distributor truck came equipped with spray bars with elbows designed to fold in on the end and then turn 90°. This is to avoid sticking out into traffic while driving.

"No sur, Missa Kinny. Dis truck a lil' fancier dan yo truck."

"Well I want to get those sprayers cleaned out too. So I'll tell you what. Pull over up there," Ken pointed to a clearing off side of the road, "I'm going to get on the back and stand on the platform while you drive the truck."

Ken climbed out of the cab, circled the truck and jumped up on the platform. John put the truck in gear and drove down the road. Safely on the back of the truck, Ken grabbed the lever opening the valve to the sprayers.

"Oh My God! John, stop the truck!

The truck heaved to full stop and John hustled to the back to see what the problem was with Missa Kenny. He had forgotten to straighten the bars out into the extended position so they sprayed him from both sides like a two-headed shower.

There he stood, dripping in asphalt from the hair on his head to the toes of his work boots. The asphalt had shot out of both sides of the sprayers, completely covering Ken in black road tar.

While he cussed up a storm, John quietly laughed to himself. Ken folded the spray bars out. Then he sprayed and emptied the last of the diesel from the truck, while his anger and frustration turned to embarrassment. He and John cleaned up the truck. Like whipped puppy, Ken walked back to the office, following behind the truck.

Ken and the distributor truck slowly trudged up the road. It didn't take long for Marve to step out of his office and watch Ken walk up behind his sparkly clean distributor truck. He laughed so hard he could barely stand up straight.

"Well, if that don't beat the band!" Marve announced.

John stepped down out of the truck and handed Marve his keys. Marve thanked John, wiping tears of laughter from his eyes.

"Missa Kinny, I am sho wishn' I had me a whole buncha feathers an a camera right now."

Papa Smurf

1968

The paving business was not the only place that Ken ended up showered in disagreeable matter. He received quite a surprise from his family during a camping outing, only a few years before being tarred with asphalt.

Ken won a bid to build the concrete footing for two 90 foot light posts located in Iowa. He and his foreman, Bill Flesher, decided to bring their families along on the trip. They all checked into a KOA campground where all of the kids could swim and enjoy other activities safely on the grounds.

Ken and Alice had prepared the '42 camping bus while Bill brought his six-pack camper and a large tent for all the kids. The sites were beautifully groomed with large fenced playgrounds for the younger kids and plenty of accessible swimming areas and walking paths for everyone else.

The night they finished setting up camp, Ken discovered he had sewage leaking from the bus septic tank. By mid-morning the next day he narrowed the problem down to a slide valve that was installed on the pipe just below the septic tank. When his attempts to open and close the valve didn't seem to solve the problem, it became obvious that he needed a replacement part.

Ever so carefully, he dumped all of the sewage out of the septic tank and rinsed the tank out with clean water and gathered the family around before heading into town for a valve.

"Whatever you do, DO NOT use the toilet in the bus," he explained to his family. "Go use the camp facilities for today. Also, DO NOT dump the contents of the toilet into the septic tank." Everyone nodded their heads in compliance.

Ken wound up driving all the way to Omaha to buy a new valve. He was gone several hours and when he returned to install the new valve he got down onto his back to wiggle under the bus.

Once positioned under the septic tank, he began to disassemble the connecting pipes; unscrewing several bolts that held the valve to the bottom of the septic tank. He held it in place while he got all the bolts out. Unfortunately, the minute he tugged on the valve to break it away from the septic tank, all of the sewage blasted down and into his face.

Ken scrambled out from under the bus, but to no avail. The entire contents of smelly blue sewage had drained from the tank, right onto his face. Not only was it incredibly disgusting to be hosed down with the family waste from the septic tank, but Ken's face would be stained for several days with bluish-green septic chemical.

Papa Smurf was on his feet; cussing up a storm in between spitting on the ground and wiping his eyes with the back of his dirty hands. He was a noisy, smelly mess. His family all scurried around to the back of the bus to investigate the ruckus; Ken was greeted with shocked faces.

The silent faces morphed and soon his family erupted into hilarious laughter.

"Who in the hell dumped that Monomatic chemical into the septic tank?" Ken hollered. Of course nobody owned up to the colossal 'mistake' resulting in the creation of this yuck-monster standing before them.

Although he never discovered who had put the chemical in the tank, Ken spent the next few days in the KOA campground posing as angry Papa Smurf, until finally, his complexion and his attitude both cleared up.

The Skunk Sweater

1973

In the middle of a hot Omaha afternoon, Ken watched John and another employee chip seal a parking lot. He decided that Lloyd, the young, tall blonde he'd hired a few weeks back, must be incredibly uncomfortable with all that long hair hanging on the back of his neck and down around his face.

The summer heat radiated off of the blacktop and the hired hands peeled off their shirts; Ken noticed the stringy locks clinging to Lloyd's sweaty chest. He couldn't keep quiet any longer.

"Say, Lloyd." Ken walked up to the two men, "What do you think about maybe getting that hair cut?" He suggested. "It would look a little better on the job and also, it wouldn't be so hot."

Lloyd stopped working and rested a lanky arm on the end of his broom handle. "Ain't nobody going to make me cut my hair!" He wiped the stringy, sweat-soaked bangs away from his forehead with the back of his forearm. "I got my rights. And I'm keeping my hair just the way I want. If you don't like it, then I'll sue you." He grabbed up his broom, the empty bucket, and then walked to the back of the distributor truck to get more asphalt.

John looked up at Ken and winked. "I take care a dis for ya, Missa Kinny."

John moved over to another large hole in the parking lot. "When youze done over there, come on an help me tack coat dis hole, Lloyd."

John had a long handled broom, twice as long as Lloyds. He waited for the smart mouthed kid to bend over the hole and he dipped the broom in the bucket and made a pass right across the kids head. Lloyd's blonde hair was clear full of asphalt.

Lloyd sputtered, cussed, and spit out asphalt all afternoon. But when he came to work the next morning, he showed up with a haircut. John and Ken watched him walk onto the parking lot.

"I gotcho back, Missa Kinny."

"I know you do, John."

By early afternoon the job was complete. Ken and John returned to the lot to clean out the distributor truck. They were in the back of the truck emptying the remaining asphalt tar, struggling with a hose that was too big to fit into a barrel, when they got an unexpected visit from Lee.

"It won't fit down in da bung of da barrel, Missa Kinny"

Ken watched John on the ground trying to maneuver the hose down inside the barrel. "Well, just put it down on top of the barrel," he pointed to the opening, "and hold it tight."

John did as he was instructed and Ken grabbed hold of the lever to open up the flow of tack coat. The thick, black tar pumped out immediately under the enormous pressure and coursed out of the truck, through the hose, and down into the container.

While the two men curiously watched the liquid goo shooting down into the barrel, Lee zipped into the lot, driving his brand-new yellow car with a white hardtop. He had been out enjoying a beautiful afternoon with his windows down. He was apparently in a good mood because Ken noticed he was wearing his favorite sweater; some furry black and white angora thing that Ken liked to call The Skunk Sweater.

Lee pulled up and parked right behind John. He got out of the car and hollered. "Hey! What in the hell are you doin' there, John?"

John turned over a shoulder to answer Lee, except he didn't leave the hose in place. Instead he turned with the hose in his hand. "Eyeez puttn' this asphalt in for –"

John doused Lee right in the face with the tar! The thick blackness squirted out of the hose not only covering Lee and his fuzzy skunk sweater, but John managed to coat Lee's white leather upholstery and his pearly white hardtop car before Ken could stop laughing long enough to shut off the valve.

"Oh John," Ken said through tears of laughter, "That's twice in one day!"

Lark 5 Amphibian

1974

Years earlier in 1968, Ken and Lee purchased the first military Amphibian vehicle from the government. The second odd-shaped, 30 foot long, propeller driven boat they ran across in the Military Surplus catalogs also came with an impressive V-8 Cummins diesel engine.

These Amphibians were called Lark 5's and unlike their predecessors, they came equipped with huge earthmover type tires; which made it efficient on land because of the four-wheel-drive and the power steering. This enabled the vehicle to turn a corner with the front wheels turned one way while the back wheels turned the opposite way. Impressively, it turned on a dime, given its considerable size.

The military used them for amphibious warfare in Vietnam and after Ken's first experience with his Amphibian, he immediately put in a bid, and got it, paying somewhere in the neighborhood of $3,000. The lark was transported from Louisiana on a flatbed. Once his new toy was operational he took it out to play. The first person he stopped to talk with, happened to be an owner of a sand pit near the little town of Valley, Nebraska.

The man allowed as how he could use Ken's new toy in his sand business. He had a dredge on a barge, located in the middle of the lake. Part of his job was to dredge up sand and deposit it on shore. Periodically, of course, mechanical issues would occur and moving equipment from the barge into his shop, which was on land, became incredibly challenging.

The Amphibian would be perfect because the drop deck was situated just above water level and the equipment could easily be slid onto the vehicle, driven on to land, and then directly into his shop.

Ken sold his Amphibian to the sand pit operator for $5,000 and began looking for another one to come up for bid. A short time later he received a bid invitation, sent it in, and was awarded another Lark.

A few days after receiving the confirmation, Ken opened up another piece of government issued mail informing him that the Larks had been placed on the ammunition list. Any equipment on the ammunition list had to be demilitarized before it could come off of the base.

For Ken, this meant he was required to make a cut completely around the hull, both directions, cutting it into quarters. Obviously this was not an appealing option, so he declined the bid.

Many years later, Ken and Alice purchased a beautiful, undeveloped piece of property west of Sekiu, Washington. Located 16 miles from the northwestern tip of the Olympic peninsula, the estate comes complete with ocean beach access.

On several occasions Ken fantasized about having a Lark to drive right off of the beach: one could simply pull the amphibian up to the front porch, climb in, and drive right off into the ocean. He could take his friends or family fishing or maneuver around on the land; it would be a perfect vehicle for his Sekiu paradise.

One day, unable to get his mind off of the amphibian, he opened up his Apple I-Pad and searched on Google for a

Lark 5. To his surprise there were several out there for sale. All were priced between $70,000 and $90,000!

He closed his I-Pad and thought to himself: *If only I had bought a bunch of those Larks and just sat on them for a few years – what a retirement I could be having right now!*

Jet Fuel & Avgas

1974

Ken considered himself a successful paving business owner by now. He had acquired an asphalt paving machine, a few dump trucks, a roller, and all of the little miscellaneous tools and equipment necessary to pave or repair parking lots. But something that bothered him was the fact he had to continually purchase asphalt from a competitor.

Mulling over his monetary inconvenience, Ken ran across an opportunity to buy an asphalt plant advertised in the military surplus catalog. They were selling an array of equipment located at the Navy Construction base in Port Hueneme, California. Ken was eager to bid at the public auction so, naturally he made the trip to the base.

He discovered that this particular auction intended to sell the many components of the plant separately, as opposed to selling it for one lump sum price. Ken came up with a plan.

He allowed as how the plant would not be good for somebody to use if it was missing one of its key components. He determined that if he bought the first item up for bid, which happened to be the aggregate dryer, he could pay almost any price for it. Then he could get the rest of the plant quite reasonably.

When the dryer came up for sale he bought it and his logic paid off. The rest of the equipment sold for incredibly low prices. Now that he had an asphalt plant located in California, he had to figure out a way to get it back to Omaha. All of the pieces except the pug mill section could be shipped by rail.

The pug mill was too high to fit on a rail car so Ken arranged to have it loaded onto a lowboy trailer. He drove it home, purchasing over-height permits in every state he went through. Additionally, he had to plan out a route avoiding bridges or overpasses under 17 feet. He managed to get all of the plant pieces to Omaha, where he rented a lot to set up for his new asphalt manufacturing business.

Assembling the plant and calibrating everything to create a superior product turned out to be an enormous challenge for Ken.

His equipment was known in the asphalt plant industry as a continuous mix plant. This meant that all of the components needed to be adjusted. The precise amounts of each of the materials had to go onto the conveyor belts, so that when they were mixed, the final product met specifications.

The asphaltic cement was stored in a tank that was heated by the hot oil heater to a temperature of 300°. Then it was pumped into the pug mill, or mixing chamber, in exactly the right amounts to continually meet mix specifications. Once Ken conquered these problems, the next step was to start paving with asphalt from his new plant.

The aggregate dryer tube measured about 30 feet long; it rotated, dumping the aggregate constantly through a 30 foot long flame. This dried all of the moisture out of the aggregate, heating it to around 300° which was then ready for mixing.

In order to produce the long flame, the dryer burned about 60 gallons of diesel fuel per hour. Add to this, the 20 gallons per hour that the hot oil heater burned, the amount of fuel consumed on any given day was horrific.

In 1974 the Arabs had stopped selling oil to the U.S. This resulted in long lines at the gas pumps and serious cutbacks by the oil companies. It also meant the amount of petroleum products they could deliver to their customers was greatly reduced. What this meant for Ken was that his diesel supplier cut him off altogether.

He found himself in a serious predicament. Without the diesel fuel to run his plant, he was out of business. Unfortunately, with the money he had borrowed to buy and build the plant, among his other business responsibilities, Ken knew going out of business was simply not an option. He had to come up with another plan.

He sure as hell couldn't get the Arabs to ship him more oil, nor could he convince the oil companies to sell him some of the oil that was rationed. There was only one thing to do: turn to the military surplus bid catalogs.

The Air Force at Offutt airbase had a tank full of salvage jet fuel. When Ken took a drive to the base to find out what *salvage jet fuel* was exactly, they informed him it was a combination of a several products. They led him out to a 30,000 gallon tank the base used for defueling aircraft and dumping used motor oil.

It turned out that the fuel in the tank was comprised of mostly jet fuel but also 120 – 140 octane aviation gas. Ken bought the entire tank of surplus fuel for two cents per gallon. The next problem was how to transport and store 30,000 gallons of fuel.

Ken spoke to a truck tanker company that normally supplied gas stations. The trucker informed him that due to the rationing several tankers were available. This meant Ken was able to rent a place to store his new fuel for several months. With his fuel situation under control, it was back to business as usual.

One task that everyone hated was lighting the flame in the big dryer every morning. The challenge was the fuel valve that had to be opened before you could light anything. It was down near the end of the dryer tube. You could only get as far away from it as your arm could reach to turn on the valve. Then the fuel vapor was to be lit with a fuel soaked rag on the end of the stick.

It was John's job to light the dryer, but every morning he complained about having to light that 30 foot flame. There was always a big huff every time it ignited, shooting flames backward from the dryer, right near his face. The new fuel mixture was a problem. It was magnified tenfold because the 120 – 140 octane avgas in the mixture was incredibly explosive.

Ken lit the dryer on the first go-around with the new fuel. The fuel ignited with an explosion that took off his eyebrows and blew him over backwards. Once it was lit Ken and John realized the next problem was going to be the clouds of black smoke. They billowed out of the dryer from dirty motor oil burning off in the mixture.

It didn't take long for the agent responsible for air quality in the Omaha area to begin visiting Ken on a regular basis. He insisted that Ken shut down his plant, which he did, as long as the man remained on the property. Once Ken saw the agent's taillights disappear, he started the plant back up again. Ken managed to fend him off long enough to completely use up the contaminated fuel and remain in business throughout the fuel crisis.

Ken eventually outgrew his interests in the asphalt business and sold the plant to a company in the Philippines, earning him a small profit. The memories and stories he earned over the years in the business far exceeded any profits he ever earned.

Hot Oil Heaters

1975

In all of the years that Ken purchased toys, vehicles, equipment, and gadgets from the military surplus, purchasing the three hot oil heaters turned out to be quite a roller-coaster ride.

Hot oil heaters were necessary in the asphalt business and Ken recently purchased a new heater for his plant. He knew how expensive they were, but he only bid $250 apiece on the Navy heaters. According to the bid request they cost the Navy about $16,000 apiece. However, they were marked as used and in poor condition.

The Navy base was located in Gulfport, Mississippi and Ken drove there to see what he had bought. It turned out that all three hot oil heaters were brand-new, packed in huge crates the size of single car garages. They were several times larger than any he had seen before and moving them was going to be terribly expensive.

As luck would have it, these heaters were manufactured from the same place as his heater. Ken knew a salesman from the manufacturing company. He placed a call to his salesman friend and told him about the hot oil heaters.

"I bought them from the government," Ken explained. "Did you ever run across a situation where somebody wanted a heater but couldn't afford your prices?"

"Oh, sure, that happens once in a while."

"I was hoping you and I could work something out," Ken offered.

The salesman agreed and managed to sell the first heater to a customer who was supposed to pay for it when it was delivered, but the final sale fell through.

That didn't discourage Ken for long because shortly after his conversation with the manufacturing salesman, the government posted a bid request for new hot oil heaters – the exact same kind that Ken was attempting to unload.

Ken submitted a bid to sell his three hot oil heaters back to the government for $12,000 apiece. He was the low bidder and subsequently awarded the bid and was certain he was going to cut fat hog in the ass on this one! Unfortunately, when the Navy figured out they were buying back the same oil heaters they had sold Ken as surplus only a month before, they rescinded the bid offer.

Eventually Ken unloaded them to private party for a decent profit. And although he took a lot less than $12,000 apiece for them, the Navy's rejection did not affect him nearly as much as he expected.

The Plant Gate

1975

Ken was always a welcomed sight on payday. One particular late afternoon he showed up to the job and motioned for his crew to come over for doughnuts and paychecks. They brought over what was left in their thermoses for a quick break with the boss.

Ken recently purchased two brand new white, single axle Chevy dump trucks with 10 foot boxes on them. He looked around for a man to fetch a final load for the day, knowing John would be the only available driver.

"John."

"Yeah, Missa Kinny?"

"Come with me so I can get you a set of keys to this new truck."

"Yes sir, Mr. Kenny." John tipped back the last swallow of coffee, screwed the cup back onto his thermos and picked up his envelope to follow Ken. Opening his envelope to peek inside at his paycheck he let out a slow, high-pitched whistle.

"What's matter, John?"

"Oh, nothing. Jus not as much as I was spectn'."

"What you mean? Hell, you don't have that many expenses." Ken reached into the cab of his truck to retrieve the keys to the Chevy dump truck. "How do you piss away so much money?" He asked John, closing the truck door.

"Oh, if you spend jus one Saturday night in my neighbahood," John giggled, "you'll never wana be white again!"

Ken busted out laughing. It wasn't often that John got one over on him. He handed the keys over and explained they were almost finished with the job so all they needed was the one load.

"I need you to hustle down there, get it, and get back to the site so they can finish it up." John put his envelope in his back pocket and nodded.

"Now dammit, John, I hate to turn you lose in my brand-new dump truck. You promise me you'll be careful."

"Awhh, Missa Kinny, I wouldn't hurt yo bran-new dump truck."

Ken handed him the keys and returned to his office anxious to finish up a bid before deadline. It wasn't long before the phone rang.

"Missa Kinny, I done had little trouble on the job."

"Jesus Christ, John! What'd you do to my new truck?"

"It wuddn't my fault, Missa Kinny, not dis time . . . I had that damn asphalt truck parked under dat pug mill. They had it shut down for jus a few minutes an they was fixing to drop a load of asphalt in dare . . . an you know they makes really big batches over at dat place . . . they put in 5 or 6 ton in one dump. . . "

"So what happened, John?"

"Well, I jus got out a da truck to get a quick smoke an I forgot to put on dat emergency brake. Naw, Missa Kenny, that sho wazn't my fault, cuz when dat asphalt come down outa dat pug mill . . . 5 ton made dat new truck a yours jump!

Ughhh . . . Ken exhaled.

". . . an it started rollin' back down da hill. You know dat man had his gates down there standin' wide open… but he didn't have it folded back like he was supposed to…

"And?"

"Well, he jus had it pointed straight open- towards da road and da truck rolled on backerds an hit dat damn gate an smashed it up into a little ball."

Looking out his office window, Ken let out another heavy sigh while John continued.

"I think you need to talk to him Missa Kinny. He's pretty mad."

When the adjuster arrived with his final assessment and paid for the gate he pulled Ken aside.

"If you let John drive your truck one more time…!"

Waking the Dead in Barstow, CA

1975

Ken purchased some military surplus trucks from the Marine Corps supply depot in Barstow, California. By this time Lee Anderson resided in the Los Angeles area with his teenage son, Mark.

For years Mark had worked for his father as a mechanic fixing forklifts and he turned out to be a pretty fair mechanic. Ken knew the trucks were in need of mechanical attention so he called Lee to find out Mark's availability.

"I've got these trucks over in Barstow to pick up and bring back to Nebraska. Is there any chance I can get Mark to come over there and help me get them running?"

"I don't have anything pressing for him. I'm sure he'd help you out."

"How about you have Mark meet me at the Marine depot?" Ken suggested. Lee agreed to pass the information along to his son.

Mark drove an old white '57 van. Ken easily spotted him driving around the lot and hailed him over. David, Ken's son, came along to drive the second truck back. All day the three men worked tirelessly on the trucks and managed to get them road worthy. With only a sliver of daylight left they checked into the Motel 6 to clean up and retire for the evening.

Ken and David bunked together while Mark inhabited the other bed. The next morning when Ken awoke, he noticed that Mark was missing. Not only was he not there in the neighboring bed, but the covers and pillows had gone missing as well.

"What happened to Mark?" Ken asked David.

"I don't know." David stretched and rolled out of bed.

While father and son primped and polished for their day, a game of 'Where's Waldo?' developed on the topic of what could have happened to Mark? Carrying their luggage out to the car, David pointed to Mark's van.

"Well, his van is here." David said.

Ken peeped through the window and identified motel blankets tussled in the back of the van. He opened the driver's side door and hollered: "Mark, you in there?"

The van rocked from one side to the other spitting Mark up inside of his cab. His eyes were swollen and bloodshot.

"What in the hell is the matter with you?" Ken asked Mark.

"Me?" Mark rubbed his eyes, "Jesus Christ - how can you snore like that and still live?"

"I don't snore." Ken lied and David laughed.

"Are you kidding?" Mark flipped the covers off his back and crawled into the driver's seat. "I was in that bed in there and I covered my head up with four pillows. I had them so tight to my head, I couldn't even breathe. There was NO WAY I could get to sleep with all that racket."

"Oh, no, Mark." Ken shook his head and laughed, continuing to deny any involvement.

"I'll be God damned if I didn't come out here and get in the van," Mark continued, "and I could still hear you clear through that brick hotel!"

Years later Mark joined the Navy. Ken arranged to visit Lee while he was in the LA area on business. Lee informed him that Mark would be down at the Navy base in San Diego all night, so he was welcome to stay in his son's bedroom. This didn't turn out to be the case and Mark came home during the middle of the night.

When Ken woke the next morning and wandered out into the living room, he discovered Mark lying on the couch with his head covered with pillows.

"Hey, Ken." A muffled greeting escaped from under the pillows. Mark uncovered his face to reveal large puffy, red eyes.

"Mark?"

"Unbelievable." Mark said to Ken. "You haven't improved a bit over the years…you were shaking the damn house. As a matter of fact, I could hear you even before I came in and I knew I'd have to sleep on the couch."

Ken laughed out loud.

"I was laying here listening to that racket and I managed to invent you an anti-snoring device."

"Ahhhh." Ken wiped his eyes, "Really, what is it?"

"I'm gunna get me one of those oxygen masks out of a jet fighter and hook it up to a Midas muffler. That'll fix you up."

A Sweet Helicopter Deal

1974

The Davis Monthan Airbase in Tucson, Arizona was known as the airplane graveyard. Over 300 helicopters were housed there waiting to be sold at auction. Ken revealed this flipping through his government surplus sealed bid invitations one evening at the Bauer dinner table. It was a discovery that would change his future.

"Would you look at this, Alice." Ken held the paper across the table for her to see. "They've got helicopters for sale at Davis Monthan Air Force Base in Tucson. They're selling 300 helicopters individually at auction.

"That is the stupidest thing I've ever heard you say!" She sat her coffee cup down hard on the table. "I can't believe you're going to buy a helicopter when you don't know anything about helicopters. You'll go over there and some will be dirty, some will be clean, and you won't know which one to buy."

"Alice." Ken interrupted his wife. "I didn't say I wanted to buy one, all I said was that they had some for sale." He held his gaze, but it could not penetrate the piercing blue eyes staring back at him. Finally, she gave in and simply huffed at his preposterous statement.

The next day Ken drove around, unable to get Alice or the helicopters out of his mind. He thought to himself, *by God I'll show her!* Ken stopped at his office and called the airlines to book a trip to Tucson.

When the time came he flew to Tucson to look at the helicopters at the airbase. They had all 300 of them lined up like pretty maids in a row. He walked down each aisle looking at them. Sure enough, some were dirty and some were clean and he didn't have any idea which helicopter to buy. *Oh, God, I hate to go home and have to admit this!* He thought to himself.

The actual sale was held at a hotel the following morning. The auctioneer referenced each helicopter by number accompanied by a picture projected up on a large screen. Ken had to come up with some kind of a scheme to figure out which was a good one to buy.

He decided to walk around the auction listening to conversations among the other bidders and locate someone who really knew helicopters. Next, he'd watch to see which birds they bid on and he would bid on the same ones. This seemed like a perfect scheme.

After some time walking around the room, listening in on conversations, two men caught his attention. *They seem to know helicopters*, he thought, and when he got in close enough to look over their shoulders one man had marked 'good' next to number 38.

Ah, ha! By God, when number 38 comes up . . . Ken thought to himself, *I'll buy that one.* He got his paddle ready and when number 38 was announced he bid on it - and got it! He paid $3,850. After the purchase Ken's curiosity got the better of him. He approached the two men.

"Say, I notice on this helicopter that I just bought you had it marked in your book as good. Can you tell me anything about it?"

"Oh, Jesus, –" the man's eyes enlarged and he shook his head at Ken, "don't go by anything we have to say." Both men were now shaking their heads at Ken. "We don't know anything about helicopters. We're in the insurance business."

Oh Shit . . . Ken continued to walk around the room and finally noticed someone in a jacket with Evergreen Helicopters embroidered on the back. The two men introduced themselves over a handshake.

"You know I just bought this helicopter, this number 38." Ken said. "What do you think about that one?"

Mr. Evergreeen, looked in his bid book and said "Just a minute, lemme look here. I don't have that one marked. I don't have any idea whether it's good or bad. Did you notice if the rotor blades were strapped to the skids?."

"Yes, I believe they were."

"Well, on some of the helicopters, the serial numbers on some of the rotor blades don't match the serial numbers in the logbooks. If that happens, you can't use those rotor blades. You'll have to buy new blades."

"What do new blades cost?" Ken asked.

"About $10,000 for the pair."

Ken felt tiny gas bubbles forming in his gut. Meanwhile, his brain released nauseous waves of guilt. Then he heard the '*I told you so*'s in Alice's voice. He had planned to purchase two helicopters but fantasy was turning to delusion by the moment. Then another thought came to him: he decided run out to the airbase and take a look at what he had bought.

When he arrived at the airbase he was surprised to see that his helicopter didn't look that bad, but it didn't look that good either - it just looked like a helicopter. He went to the main office to retrieve the logbook for the craft. He looked through the pages and came to the serial number for the blades. They didn't match the numbers stamped onto the blades tied to the skids.

Oh, my God - what am I going to do now? The worst part was facing Alice. He'd probably have to leave his helicopter behind and then try to explain how on Earth he managed to piss away $3,850.

This was a real problem.

Ken flipped through the logbook, pondering the conundrum he'd gotten himself into and on the very last page there was a notation about a change of rotor blades. Those serial numbers matched the serial numbers on the blades that were tied to the skids on his ship.

Whoowho! Ken did a happy dance in his head. He'd crashed landed right into another outhouse – and come out smelling like a rose!

He returned home to locate a flatbed trailer to pull behind his station wagon in order to retrieve his new toy. He brought his friend and paving foreman, Dick Stimson, along. Dick was quite a character. Just a few weeks ago he'd shown up to work with his neck bandaged.

"Dick, what the hell happened to you?" Ken asked when he showed up on the job site.

"Well, me and this pretty little black gal hit it off at the bar last night and we went back to her place." This happened frequently to Dick, only this time the gal was married. Her husband arrived just as Dick climbed into his car and started the engine. The driver side window was down and the husband pulled out a .25 caliber automatic and shot Dick through the neck.

"Thank God I had the car started when he showed up."

"He actually shot you?" Ken asked.

"Ya, he shot me right through my neck - I barely had time to get the car in drive and get the hell out of there. I drove to the hospital before I bled to death!" The hospital ran x-rays; the bullet had gone clear through his neck and out the other side of the car. They bandaged his wound and turned him loose. Dick came to work a few hours later, still drunk and with the bandages on his neck.

When Ken and Dick arrived at Davis Monthan Airbase, they loaded his bird. On the way home they stopped at Tate's ranch, in Demming, New Mexico near the Mexican border.

Later that evening they checked into a local motel. The motel was located just down the street from a cowboy bar playing very loud, country and western music. Dick decided to visit the bar while Ken went to bed.

The next morning when Ken got up he saw Dick sleeping in the bed next to him. Dick and the bed were covered in blood. It looked as if somebody was murdered there. Dick's eyes were both swollen shut, his nose and mouth were bleeding, and he had bruises all over his body.

"Dick, what the hell happened you? Can you even get up out of bed? How bad do you think you're hurt?"

"I really feel like hell, but I think I'll make it all right." Dick answered.

"What happened?" Ken asked his friend.

"Some cowboys in that bar I went to last night seemed to take offense at my dancing with one of their women. Three of them beat the living shit out of me. Then, when they got me on the ground, they put the boots to me. I hurt all over." Dick slowly crawled out of out of bed and made his way into the shower. The two of them headed for Tate's house.

"What in the hell happened to you?" Tate asked. "Oh, I got the shit kicked out of me in the bar last night. I guess I'm going to have to quit fooling around with other guys' women."

"Oh," Ken and Tate exchanged looks again; Ken shook his head, raised his eyebrows and opted to say nothing.

Before heading back home to Omaha, Ken made a trip to a little Mexican border town across from Tate's place. Due to a sugar shortage, Ken received strict orders from Alice to bring some sugar back from Mexico.

He purchased three 50 lb bags of sugar but had nowhere to put them once they hooked up the trailer with the helicopter on it. The sugar bags weighed too much for the back of the station wagon. The weight on the hitch was already maxed out carrying the helicopter. So Ken found a place for them snugged down beneath the belly of the helicopter, on the deck of the trailer.

"Looks good, boss. Let's go!" Dick said, anxious to have New Mexico in his rearview mirror.

Once they were on the road Ken had another issue to address: the gasoline shortage. It was getting late in the evening and several of the gas stations were already closed. Ken worried he would be unable to get enough gas to make it home. The station wagon bobbed up and down from the weight of the helicopter each time Dick hit a rut in the road. Ken got an idea!

"We'll stop and fill up the wagon and the helicopter gas tank and that way we could drain it out if we needed it."

While Dick filled up the station wagon gas tank, Ken pumped gas into the helicopter. He wasn't sure but he thought he could hear something trickling; he became certain the minute he smelled the gas. Ken knelt down and looked under his new bird. A drain valve on the bottom of the helicopter was open and the gasoline was draining down onto the sugar.

Ughhhh!

Ken stopped the pump, closed the drain, and then filled the tank back up. After paying for the gas, the two men headed for home.

Driving through the night, Ken pondered Alice's reaction. Was she going to be more upset with him over her gasoline soaked sugar or the fact he had just come home with a helicopter?

Ken brought the helicopter home, with the intention of reselling it. He placed several ads in "Trade a Plane" and got no response. He thought the problem was more than likely its present condition.

Moreover, it did not qualify for an airworthiness certificate from the FAA. Without this certificate, the helicopter could not be flown for any civilian use even if it was in new condition. In order to get one, all of the time change parts had to have times verified. This meant the helicopter had to be disassembled.

Ken went to visit the aircraft mechanic instructor at Iowa Western College in Council Bluffs.

"Do you have any students close to graduation? Someone ready and willing to work on my helicopter?" Ken asked Earl, the college instructor.

"What kind of helicopter do you have?"

"I have a military version called an OH 23. The civilian designation is Hiller 12-D."

"You've got to be the luckiest guy in the world. I have that exact same helicopter here at the school and my students disassemble and reassemble it every semester," Earl told Ken. "They're not real sharp yet on other kinds of aircraft, but they really know this one."

"Do you have a particular student that I could hire?"

"Yes, I believe I do. I have a student that has already passed his airframe examination and is working on his engine rating. It would be legal for him to work on your airframe now and do the engine after he receives his engine rating. I'll have Larry Blackman call you."

When Larry called, Ken invited him to look at the helicopter which was in his garage at home. Larry allowed as how he could make the helicopter look and fly like new.

"What would you charge me to do that?" Ken asked.

"Well, uh . . . would six dollars an hour be too much?"

Ken agreed to the price and told Larry that he would give him a nice bonus on top of his wages if he did a really nice job. He also told him that it would be okay for Larry to work any hours he had available, including weekends and after school.

Larry started the next weekend by disassembling the helicopter in Ken's garage. He had helicopter pieces, large and small, scattered all over. When Ken saw his helicopter laying in pieces, he thought it was a goner. He had no idea where all of those pieces would fit. Larry assured him that he had everything under control and that he would have the helicopter looking like new in a short time.

Larry thoroughly cleaned every piece, stripping the paint off, replacing any necessary parts, and then he painted them with DuPont Imron paint. As he began to put all of these parts back together, it started looking more and more like a helicopter. When he had the fuselage finished and the instrument panel replaced with new or refurbished instruments, Larry reinstalled the newly upholstered seat.

After the seat was in place, Ken and his seven-year-old son Kenny tried to learn how to fly the helicopter. Ken sat in the seat behind the controls with a flight manual in hand, and moved the controls like he was actually flying the helicopter. Kenny made the engine noise at the appropriate times. They spent hour after hour playing with their new toy.

By and by, Larry got the helicopter completely painted and reassembled. When it came time to actually run the helicopter, of course they had to move it out of the garage.

They found, and marked, the exact sweet spot on the driveway where the whirling rotor blades would miss Ken's front porch, the neighbor's porch, and a big tree in his front yard.

Running the helicopter often attracted the neighbors and passersby. When they made adjustments to the engine or tracked the rotor blades, there would always be strange cars parked across the street and down the block.

Once Larry was finished with the helicopter he invited his school instructor to come see his accomplishments. Earl was really impressed and confirmed he would be giving Larry an "A" for his fine work.

"What are you going to do with it, now?" Earl asked Ken.

"I think I'll fly it out of here and park it at the airport."

"You've got to be joking. How many flying hours do you actually have?" Earl asked.

"I don't really have any actual flying hours in a helicopter, but Kenny and I have been studying the flight manual and dry-flying the helicopter in the garage for the last two months."

"I have over 200 flying hours in a helicopter just like this one. I wouldn't try flying it out of a place this tight." Earl said. "Please don't try this. You're going to break a really nice helicopter and probably your neck at the same time."

Ken finally hauled the helicopter on a flatbed trailer to the South Omaha airport. Larry and Earl met him there and immediately began flight tests; making final adjustments to ensure the aircraft was safe to fly.

"Do you want to try to fly this thing?" Earl asked.

"Sure I can fly it. No problem." Ken retorted, with confidence. After all, he'd been flying airplanes for years. How tough could it be?

The two men strapped on their seat-belts and with the dual controls in their hands, Earl asked, "You wouldn't happen to be a betting man would you, Ken?"

"Sure, what do you want to bet?"

"I'll bet you a case of beer that you crash within the first five seconds."

"That's a bet!" Ken said, thinking this was going to be the easiest case of beer he ever earned.

Earl picked up the helicopter to a 4 foot hover and told Ken, "She's all yours." When Ken tried his hand at the controls the helicopter went crazy. He would've crashed in about two seconds if Earl hadn't saved the day.

"That's not fair," whined Ken, "you had your hands on the controls and did something."

"Okay" Earl said, "I'll bring her up to about a 10 foot hover and I'll take my hands off of the controls. Would you like to bet another case of beer? Same bet?"

"Okay, only this time I'm going to win." Said Ken with slightly less confidence. The same thing happened the second time. He allowed as how maybe he should take some flying lessons from Earl.

Ken spent hour after hour without being able to hover and finally asked Earl what he was doing wrong.

"Learning to hover a helicopter is a little like learning to ride a pogo stick in a room full of ball bearings. It takes lots of practice." After about seven hours of lessons, Ken felt like he was beginning to get the feel of it.

One Sunday morning, Earl didn't show up to give Ken his lesson. Ken thought just maybe, he could lift up on the collective just a little bit and scoot the helicopter along the ground far enough to reach the fuel pad and refuel. This worked out for him, so he scooted it back. After that successful maneuver, Ken decided to try and hover just above the tops of the grass.

Because he was having such a good day on his own, he decided to bring it up to a 4 foot hover. He hovered the helicopter around the airport for about another hour, at which time he flew the helicopter around the airport several times. He was absolutely amazed and extremely proud of being able to finally fly the helicopter.

Ken called Alice from the airport office and told her to get to the airport as quickly as she could and bring the movie camera. When Alice showed up he gave her a quick demonstration of his new flying prowess. She captured the antics on film for posterity.

That same morning, Ken's daughter Sherri and her friend, Debbie, showed up at the airport to see her father finally fly his helicopter.

"I'm getting really good at this, would you like to go for a ride?" The girls both jumped into the helicopter, which unbeknownst to Ken, made the helicopter overweight. The weight plus the high density altitude, caused by the hot weather, was about to cause Ken to have his first helicopter hard landing.

Ken revved up the engine to full power and lifted the helicopter off the ground where it immediately went into forward flight. His flight path took him over the top of a parked airplane. All of a sudden the engine rpm's began to bleed off and the helicopter started to come down.

At first Ken thought he was going to hit the parked airplane, but luckily he got past it before he actually hit the ground, hard. Both doors popped open and the girls bailed out. Ken thought they look like rats deserting a sinking ship. Sherri would never fly with her father again for the next three years.

Ken learned a valuable lesson about thinking he was a better pilot than he really was. Luckily, no one was hurt and the helicopter was not damaged. When Ken told Earl about his flying adventure over the weekend, Earl was livid.

"You idiot, do you realize how many FAA regulations, not to mention laws, you broke with that fiasco? You might easily have killed your daughter and her girlfriend, not to mention yourself. You don't even know how to make an auto rotation yet. If that engine had quit, you'd all be dead now."

Ken went back to his lessons and really learned to fly the helicopter properly. This would soon pay off for him and his family.

In 1975, a large tornado struck Omaha causing considerable damage in the west part of the city.

"It's too bad you don't have your commercial helicopter license," Alice commented. "I'll bet you could make a lot of money flying helicopter sightseeing rides over the tornado area." Ken allowed as how that was a great idea.

He drove to the Westroads Shopping Center to speak with the manager, knowing their heliport was only used once a year to bring in Santa Claus. He made a deal with the manager to fly helicopter rides over the tornado area from their heliport.

Ken agreed to collect $5 per person to cover the pilot's costs plus any donations to the Salvation Army tornado relief fund. Alice taped down the plastic lid of a 2lb coffee can, cut a slit in the top, and this is how Ken collected the donations.

Ken hired a commercial helicopter pilot, bought some carnival-ride style tickets, and began flying helicopter rides from the Westroads heliport. The ad he and Alice placed in the newspaper brought a flood of people out seeking helicopter rides. The operation was a huge success until they began getting a number of complaints from the residents under the helicopter's flight path.

Ken changed the flight path over the farmer's fields west of Omaha. He surmised this would be the end of his little tornado touring business.

Surprisingly, his customers continued to show great enthusiasm to experience a helicopter ride. Ken continued to sell tickets, while his commercial helicopter pilot flew the rides. When the novelty of this operation wore off, Ken moved his operation to a county fair in Missouri Valley, Iowa. That seemed to work as well. Ken put his asphalt business on hold for the winter while he tried this new venture.

Ken made a deal with a local department store chain that had locations all around Nebraska, Iowa, and Kansas. They would pay him $1,000 per week to fly helicopter rides from the parking lots of each of their various stores. He would give each store manager 100 tickets to give out to their customers for free rides for promotion value. For all other customers, Ken charged five dollars per ride.

At a location in Kansas, Ken had Santa Claus flown in for a Christmas promotion. It snowed all weekend and every time the snow would let up enough for them to be able to see the grain elevator on the edge of town, they would fly. Ken could see that this was the wrong time of the year to conduct this kind of operation in the Midwest.

He loaded his helicopter onto his trailer, pulled by his new Chevy pickup, and drove to Arizona to visit his parents for Christmas. They lived in a mobile home park in Mesa with a patch of open, undeveloped desert across the street. Ken flew his helicopter off of the trailer and parked it in the desert area. Meanwhile, back in Omaha, Alice loaded the kids and gifts into the station wagon and headed south to Mesa.

Ken and Alice flew over the Superstition Mountains everyday looking for the lost Dutchman gold mine, with no luck. Every time he would fire up the helicopter the seniors living at the trailer court came out to watch him fly. Many of them begged Ken to fly them over the Superstition Mountains, but of course he couldn't do that yet because he didn't have his commercial helicopter license.

Ultimately, Ken made a deal with the owners of a restaurant. They had a location right next to Superstition Mountain where he could fly rides from their parking lot.

Ken hired a new commercial helicopter pilot named Tom Beber, to fly these rides. His new pilot flew the helicopter over the desert to get the "feel" of it. He made the mistake of practicing an auto rotation all the way to the ground. He hit hard and the rotor blades flexed downward enough to chop the tail boom in half. Ken removed the tail boom from the helicopter and took it to a repair station in Camarillo, California.

This boondoggle cost Ken about $5,000. When the helicopter was repaired, they started flying rides over the Superstition Mountains from the restaurant parking lot.

This operation was making money but the state of Arizona closed it down. It seemed that in Arizona, a certificate of public convenience and necessity was required for such an operation.

Christmas vacation was over for Ken's children, so Alice took them back to Omaha. Ken decided to drive the pickup, pulling his helicopter, back to Omaha via Las Vegas. He wanted to see if there might be some flying opportunities in Nevada.

And boy, was there ever!

Join us in Volume II for more Misguided Adventures of Ken Bauer.

Acknowledgements

This book was made possible by the encouragement, assistance, and support of the following people:

To all of those individuals who told Ken, *"You have the best stories. You should write a book!"*

To David Bauer, for designing the final book jacket for his grandfather.

To Buffy Naillon and Thom Hollis, for all of their hard work and talented efforts on previous jacket covers. And especially to Thom – for making the final book cover happen on a moment's notice.

To our friends and family, who sat through multiple versions as the stories were being developed. Both Ken and I appreciate your indulgence and sincere laughter through eight months worth of readings and revisions.

To Kenny, who assisted with re-writes, suggestions, contributions, and development on his father's book.

And to Alice, for her relentless pursuit of typo's, misspellings, grammar errors, and historical accuracy. We are incredibly grateful for the multiple reviews and the time you invested in assisting us with the finalization of our project.